DEVIL'S ADVOCATES

DEVIL'S ADVOCATES is a series of books devoted to exploring the classics of horror cinema. Contributors to the series come from the fields of teaching, academia, journalism and fiction, but all have one thing in common: a passion for the horror film and a desire to share it with the widest possible audience.

'The admirable Devil's Advocates series is not only essential – and fun – reading for the serious horror fan but should be set texts on any genre course.'
Dr Ian Hunter, Reader in Film Studies, De Montfort University, Leicester

'Auteur Publishing's new Devil's Advocates critiques on individual titles... offer bracingly fresh perspectives from passionate writers. The series will perfectly complement the BFI archive volumes.' **Christopher Fowler,** *Independent on Sunday*

'Devil's Advocates has proven itself more than capable of producing impassioned, intelligent analyses of genre cinema... quickly becoming the go-to guys for intelligent, easily digestible film criticism.' *Horror Talk.com*

'Auteur Publishing continue the good work of giving serious critical attention to significant horror films.' *Black Static*

 DevilsAdvocatesbooks

 DevilsAdBooks

DEVIL'S ADVOCATES

SAW

BENJAMIN POOLE

Acknowledgments

For my parents, who never allowed me to watch horror films, making them seem illicit and special; and for Deborah and Jezel, who do.

First published in 2012, reprinted 2014 by
Auteur, 24 Hartwell Crescent, Leighton Buzzard LU7 1NP
www.auteur.co.uk
Copyright © Auteur 2012

Series design: Nikki Hamlett at Cassels Design
Set by Cassels Design www.casselsdesign.co.uk
Printed and bound by CPI Group (UK) Ltd, Croydon, CR0 4YY

British Library Cataloguing-in-Publication Data
A catalogue record for this book is available from the British Library

ISBN 978-1-906733-56-8
ISBN 978-1-906733-97-1 (e-book)

CONTENTS

INTRODUCTION

Life is a horror story. It begins in uncertain shadows, brutally punctured with a bloody, painful shock; sound-tracked by screams. To live is to survive, to face and conquer threat and fear, to avoid the monster for as long as our running time will allow. But life, like all horror stories, always ends with a final scene of death.

By its very nature, the horror text tackles themes and subjects that are inherently transgressive of social norms, yet are intrinsic to the human condition. It is pop culture's own penicillin, a medicine obtained from decay which, taken in the right dose, can inoculate us from fear. We turn to horror to understand ourselves. Is it our fears we see on the screen? Is it our transgressions? Is it *ourselves*?

E.C. Comics' The Vault of Horror *circa 1950*

The genre's ideological conservatism has been well documented: victims are rarely entirely 'innocent' in horror. From early folk tales that culminated in death and bloodshed, there is a trenchant morality preached from the horror text's shadowy narratives. Primitive societies used horror narratives to control their children: *'This is what happens when you wander from the path; you could end up wolf-ravaged, like that little girl in the red hood.'* The EC comics of the 1950s would enact gruesome karma upon petty thieves and adulterers, while Victorian tales such as *The Monkey's Paw* by WW Jacobs were cautionary tales about greed.

Horror has flourished within Judeo-Christian societies, whose religions co-opt pagan mythologies to reinforce their particular brand of morality and didacticism. Carol Clover notes that 'in the slasher film, sexual transgressions of both sexes are scheduled for early destruction … postcoital death, above all when the circumstances are illicit, is a staple of the genre'. [1] After all, who is Jason Voorhees of the *Friday the 13th* cycle if not a hulking personification of parental moral majority, skewering transgression and spoiling fun (don't have sex, put down that beer)? Horror's golden ages, or, at least, periods where audiences have been most interested in the genre, can be linked to conservative governments, including Nixon's (USA, 1969–74), and Thatcher's (UK, 1979–90) presiding over the 'video nasty' era. The years where the SAW films thrived were during the Bush administration (USA, 2001–9), which became inextricably linked with images of torture in the execution (as it were) of its foreign policy.

SAW (2004) is a horror film that is entirely representative of the era that created it: the early twenty-first century witnessed a threatened America whose national confidence was shattered, and shady Middle Eastern wars played out in abject images of torture and suffering. Like the aeons of horror tales that precede it, the film is an essay in morality as well as mortality; its antagonist cleaves to a logical, if bloody moral code, while no victim is wholly without guilt. As with all of the best horror, *SAW* is interested in the spiritual and physical potential of the human body and soul: in no other genre are we more aware of our humanity, our weak bodies and their fleshy limits. This aspect of gratification, being viscerally confronted with our own mortality, is abundantly evident in the gross extremities of *SAW*'s survival horror. The particular focus is sadism and body trauma, which the film details with surgical precision.

It is typical of horror to centralise the narrative around its antagonist. Although we only glimpse Jigsaw for a few brief moments at the end of *SAW*, he is the film's plot trigger. He is *SAW*'s conscience. While Jigsaw's backstory will be mined for further exposition in subsequent films, in the first movie he is a shadowy, off-screen presence: *SAW*'s drama is centered on the victims' suffering and their futile endeavours to escape Jigsaw's games. These are constructed to suit the horror genre's ethical code of retribution; each participant has been caught not only by Jigsaw, but their own moral failings. Suffering from terminal cancer, which is in itself inescapable, Jigsaw sees the traps as beneficial to his victims; if they survive their near-death experience, they will no longer take life for granted. 'How much blood will you shed to stay alive?' is the question he intones in the first of his many grave monologues, demonstrating that at its dark heart, SAW maintains the über theme of horror – survival.

The sociological studies of the behavioural specialist Dr Marvin Zuckerman ascertain that a high proportion of horror fans are characteristically 'high sensation seekers'.[2] The cinema of SAW is one that manipulates and invokes intense audience identification, resulting in a cathartic experience. Zuckerman maintains that the horror demographic consists of males in their late-teens to mid-twenties who call for increasingly intensive thrills, or 'hits', with each horror experience. For fans, the experience of this sort of fear is itself addictive, which goes some way to account for the continued success of the franchise: consequently, each new SAW sequel must deliver to this accumulative demand, and does so; with bigger deaths and more visceral gore.

PLOT OUTLINE

Dr Lawrence Gordon (Cary Elwes), an oncologist, and Adam (Leigh Whannell), a photographer, are abruptly awoken at opposite ends of a rank, abandoned bathroom within some sort of unidentified industrial establishment. The men are fixed to the pipes with thick steel chains of about four feet in length. There is a third presence in the room, an apparently dead body lying between the two captives, holding a revolver and a microcassette recorder. A pool of blood appears to have oozed from the body's head.

Dr Gordon and Adam find audiotapes in their pockets, containing specific instructions for each. Adam has to try to escape the bathroom, while Dr Gordon's task is to kill Adam before the clock reaches 6:00, or his wife, Alison (Monica Potter), and child, Diana (Makenzie Vega), will die.

Dr Gordon believes that their captor is the 'Jigsaw Killer', an infamous serial killer whose modus operandi involves placing victims in convoluted traps, which, as his name would imply, Jigsaw refers to as 'games'. The traps usually pertain toward a perceived flaw within their personality, and put their 'players' through physical and/or psychological torture to survive. Jigsaw's philosophy is that if they 'beat' the trap, they will emerge as better people, earning a new appreciation for life.

We see two victims of Jigsaw's games in rapid flashback: Paul (Mike Butters), forced to crawl through a cage crammed with razor wire, and Mark (Paul Gutrecht), locked in a small room, his body smeared with a flammable substance – he is immolated as he uses a candle to negotiate his cell. We also meet Amanda (Shawnee Smith), the sole survivor of Jigsaw's traps; she claims that the Jigsaw experience 'helped' her.

Adam (Leigh Whannell) reaches in vain for the tape recorder

In a flashback we are made privy to the Gordons' relationship; it is distant and their child is clearly affected by this. It also emerges that Gordon is treating a terminal patient called John Kramer (Tobin Bell), whom an orderly named Zep (Michael Emerson) finds 'interesting'.

Via mobile phone, Dr Gordon is informed that their captor is holding his family hostage. Themes of voyeurism abound: as the imprisoner watches Adam and Dr Gordon through closed-circuit television, the Gordon homestead is being watched by Detective Tapp (Danny Glover), a detective who came close to apprehending Jigsaw, but has since been discharged. Tapp has begun to obsess over Dr Gordon, who he feels is somehow implicated in Jigsaw's crimes, having found Gordon's penlight at the scene of a Jigsaw murder.

Adam and Dr Gordon begin to recall how they were kidnapped: both were set upon and knocked out by a strange figure wearing robes and a pig mask. As the plot develops, it transpires that the doctor illicitly met one of his students in a seedy motel, but did not have sex with her. Under duress, Adam admits that he was paid by Detective Tapp to take photographs of the doctor as he visited the motel.

It becomes apparent that it is the orderly, Zep, who holds Dr Gordon's family prisoner. Zep makes a move to kill Alison, but she overcomes him. Tapp is alerted by the commotion. He rushes to the house and rescues Alison and Diana from Zep, chasing him to the sewers, and to the warehouse where Gordon and Adam are being held.

SAW reaches its conclusion as Dr Gordon, hearing gunshots and screaming at the end of the phone, is severely electrocuted by the ankle chain, causing him to drop the phone out of his reach. In desperation, he saws off his foot to release himself. Seemingly fulfilling the rules of the game, Dr Gordon then shoots Adam with the revolver.

Zep shoots Tapp dead and enters the bathroom with the purpose of killing Dr Gordon, but he is surprised by Adam, who is only wounded, and who proceeds to beat him to death. Dr Gordon promises his cellmate that he will come back with help, and painfully crawls away.

Adam finds another microcassette recording and plays it. It emerges that Zep was not the 'Jigsaw Killer' but just another victim of the game, playing in order to acquire the antidote for the slow poison within his body. As Adam listens to the tape, the 'corpse' in the bathroom stands to its feet, revealing itself to be John Kramer, the actual 'Jigsaw Killer'. He casually tells Adam that the key to his chain was in the bathtub, which Adam accidentally drained when he knocked out the plug in the film's opening scene. Grabbing Zep's gun, Adam attempts to shoot Jigsaw, but Jigsaw electrocutes him before he can fire. Jigsaw turns off the bathroom's lights and shuts the door, sealing Adam inside the bathroom to die.

FOOTNOTES

1. Clover, 1993: 33
2. www.bigthink.com/ideas/17531

PRODUCTION

BACKGROUND

A distasteful idea…

http://movies.nytimes.com/2007/10/27/movies/27saw.html

… vile filth

http://chicago.metromix.com/movies/movie_review/movie-review-saw-iv/243237/content

… eyeball-poppingly repulsive sadism

http://www.guardian.co.uk/film/2009/oct/15/saw-horror-movie-franchise

… cheerfully gruesome

http://rogerebert.suntimes.com/apps/pbcs.dll/article?AID=/20041028/REVIEWS/40923005/1023

The first SAW feature film received its premiere at the Sundance Film Festival in 2004. The film was received with the sort of critical acclaim that is rare for a genre film; the director of the Sundance festival, Geoffrey Gilmore, opined proudly that the horror film was 'bold, cleverly constructed and flat out terrifying', but also that the film was instilled with a 'moral seriousness'.[3] It was a triumphant finale to what had been a turbulent production history. The film was initially conceived and filmed as a short by its creators, James Wan and Leigh Whannell, in order to create a 'calling card' for potential backers. The ten-minute mini-film was a version of a particularly gruesome scene from the final SAW screenplay: the short depicted Whannell, his head surrounded by a mechanical 'bear trap', searching through a comatose man's stomach for the key to the cranial device (the scene would eventually feature Shawnee Smith in the Whannell role). The short was circulated around studios; Whannell and Wan's initial aspirations were humble, hoping that the short would show enough promise to be developed into a direct-to-video feature. However, backers were suitably impressed, and the two received enough capital to expand SAW into a full-length cinema release.

Wan and Whannell developed the *SAW* short into a feature for just $1,200,000, and after the Sundance premiere the expanded, finished film was bought by the independent studio Lionsgate to distribute worldwide. *SAW*'s success was global: it was released in every major territory (the Mexican title for the film is, brilliantly, *Juego Macabro* or *The Macabre Game*). The film went on to gross $103,096,345 worldwide, from an impressive Halloween opening weekend of $18,276,468.[4] This is a princely profit for such a steadfastly 'genre' text and ensured that a sequel was inevitable; plans were made for a spin off when the opening weekend figures of *SAW* were announced. At the time of writing, there have been six sequels in the *SAW* series; as well as a comic book, a computer game, extensive merchandise, and even a rollercoaster ride, making *SAW* a bona-fide franchise. *SAW* is the most profitable of any film series, and, for half a decade, set a new paradigm in horror cinema.

Screenwriter Leigh Whannell stars in the original SAW short

Although the popularity of the *SAW* films has now dwindled from the heady box office of *SAW III* (which made Lionsgate $164,874,275 in 2009), niche audiences have consistently returned to follow the misadventures of Jigsaw each Halloween, and, in 2010, the franchise was inducted into the Guinness Book of Records as 'the most successful horror movie series'.[5]

HISTORY

It is interesting to consider how such an apparently humble text as *SAW*, one that
propagates such abject, extreme imagery, has caught the public imagination. Like other
game-changing horror successes, such as *The Night of the Living Dead* (1968) or *The
Texas Chain Saw Massacre* (1974), or, most conspicuously, *The Blair Witch Project* (1999),
SAW's budget was, by Hollywood standards, very low ($1,200,000, compared to a
contemporary average of $33,000,000). However, low-budget successes are familiar
to horror, with fans expectant of, and even encouraged by, a film's lowly roots. The
dearth of capital can often work in the horror genre's favor. The impoverished finances
of these films are offset by the edgy sense of urgency such a rough-and-ready delivery
entails. The *mise-en-scène* in these films often has a rougher, harsher look than in their
Hollywood counterparts, and performances are similarly bluff (and often amateur); a
coarse alloy that enhances the impact of the genre, and creates verisimilitude, almost
as if the texts draw an earthy power from their budgetary restrictions. *SAW* simply
looks unpleasant; and the (at times) awkward performance codes of Whannell suit the
wretched situation his character is in.

The distributors of *SAW* were quick to capitalise on the film's genre appeal. Lionsgate
released the film, and every subsequent sequel, on the weekend before Halloween. This
savvy marketing strategy imbued each film with the aura of an 'event' release. Halloween
is an increasingly lucrative market for all commercial avenues; $235m is estimated to
have been spent in 2010 on merchandise and media linked to the 'holiday' date (twenty
times what was spent in 2001). For Hollywood it is a money-spinning half-way mark that
bridges the seasonal blockbusters of summer and winter. (One of the most successful
independent films ever was tailor-made to the iconography of this evening, and even
named after it: 1978's *Halloween*.)

The impact of *SAW* on the genre industry is discernible in the extreme horror films that
followed on from its success, films that emphasised their gory content and focused on
themes of pain and suffering. *The Guardian*'s film section acknowledged the influence
of *SAW* and the subgenre it inspired: 'Given the sheer, ruptured-sewage-pipe deluge of
gore, mutilation and general unpleasantness that has come to comprise the peculiar
sub-genre of horror known as "torture porn" [of which the writer proposes the

birthdate is the cinematic release of *SAW*] it seems hard to believe that it is barely half a decade old'.[6] Unquestionably, the film has been responsible for many imitators. One of the more interesting *SAW* cash-ins is Tom Shankland's *WΔZ* (2007), which parallels *SAW*'s intent, right down to its mirror-image title. In *WΔZ*, victims of a sadistic moral crusader are forced to choose between killing themselves or a loved one. Indeed, the trope of pinioned and punished protagonist has infected even the most mainstream of franchises; when MGM wanted to reboot a grittier Bond, they were sure to include a scene in *Casino Royale* (2006) where Bond is strapped to a chair and is whipped in an exceptionally excruciating manner. *The Dark Knight*'s (2008) antagonist ties two betrothed victims to chairs surrounded by explosives: they are linked to each other by radio signals, and the audience watch as they say their harrowing farewells to each other.

British 'Quad' for SAW II

The *SAW* film's taglines are always mindful of their audience; 'How much blood will you shed to survive?', 'We dare you again', etc. This mode of address is not simply the hyperbole of advertising; part of the squeamish pleasure of the *SAW* films is its games, with which the audience can interact on an imaginative level, probing common fears of claustrophobia and loss of control. The films are committed to engendering a conspiratorial identification between protagonists and audience.

FOOTNOTES

3. www.lionsgatepublicity.com/epk/saw5/docs/pro_notes.doc
4. www.boxofficemojo.com
5. Guiness Book of World Records, 2010
6. www.guardian.co.uk/film/2010/aug/28/torture-porn-frightfest-quiz

THE HORROR FILM AND THE STUDIO SYSTEM

Horror has an ambivalent relationship with mainstream cinema. It is a niche pleasure that is at times actively avoided by audiences who otherwise love all aspects of cinema. Indeed, critic Mark Kermode argues that there is 'an absolute divide between horror fans and everyone else in the world'.[7]

If we look at the 20 top-grossing films, then none could comfortably be classified as explicitly falling within the horror genre. To achieve mainstream success, a film must be open to large, family audiences (to accomplish 'chart-busting' box office), and horror's content and prohibitive certification would preclude this.

Rank	Title	Worldwide Box Office
1	Avatar (2009)	$2,782,300,000
2	Titanic (1997)	$1,843,200,000
3	Harry Potter and the Deathly Hallows: Part 2 (2011)	$1,328,100,000
4	Transformers: Dark of the Moon (2011)	$1,123,700,000
5	The Lord of the Rings: The Return of the King (2003)	$1,119,900,000
6	Pirates of the Caribbean: Dead Man's Chest (2006)	$1,066,200,000
7	Toy Story 3 (2010)	$1,063,200,000
8	Pirates of the Caribbean: On Stranger Tides (2011)	$1,043,900,000
9	Alice in Wonderland (2010)	$1,024,300,000
10	The Dark Knight (2008)	$1,001,900,000
11	Harry Potter and the Philosopher's/Sorcerer's Stone (2001)	$974,800,000
12	Pirates of the Caribbean: At World's End (2007)	$963,400,000
13	Harry Potter and the Deathly Hallows: Part 1 (2010)	$956,400,000
14	The Lion King (1994; 2011 3-D re-issue)	$945,700,000
15	Harry Potter and the Order of the Phoenix (2007)	$939,900,000
16	Harry Potter and the Half-Blood Prince (2009)	$934,400,000
17	The Lord of the Rings: The Two Towers (2002)	$926,000,000
18	Star Wars: Episode I - The Phantom Menace (1999)	$924,300,000
19	Shrek 2 (2004)	$919,800,000
20	Jurassic Park (1993)	$914,700,000

http://boxofficemojo.com/alltime/world/ (as at 31 December 2011; figures rounded to nearest $100,000)

Interestingly, however, it could still be argued that almost all of the films in the top 20 *do* share elements of the fantastic or even the supernatural, which are characteristically the concerns of horror. The only exception to this rule is *Titanic*, and even that film features scenes of threat and death. There are men in masks causing bloody chaos (*The Dark Knight* and *Spider-Man 3*), and monsters abound (*Pirates of the Caribbean*, *Harry Potter*, *Lord of the Rings*). Judging by the chart, it seems that despite horror's niche status, mass audiences are drawn to supernatural elements and themes of peril as a matter of course.

Nonetheless, it is relatively rare for the major studios to fund and distribute out-and-out horror films. For the most part, the films in the top 20 enjoy the creative and distributive benefits of a vertically and horizontally integrated system. For example, *The Dark Knight* is produced and distributed by TimeWarner: each stage of the film's manufacture – production, distribution and exhibition– is owned by this company (vertical integration). TimeWarner is a major media conglomerate, which owns many media outlets such as the *Time Inc* publishing company and the *CW Television Network*, allowing the company a diverse and powerful command of the marketplace. However, the types of films that benefit from this system are those that are considered investments for the studio – films that procure mass audiences and multiple revenue streams.

This is not to say that the studio system has not colluded to generate financially successful horror and horror that was 'approved' by the industry through sanctioned awards: *Rosemary's Baby* (1968) won an Oscar, and, in 1974, *The Exorcist* became the highest grossing film of all time (until it was deposed a year later by another horror, *Jaws* [1975]). It is also important to note that Universal studios were the original studio brand in horror films. Coinciding with the new technological developments of the 1930s – sound, safer and more effective film stock – the Universal studio released *Dracula* and *Frankenstein* (both 1931) in quick succession, going on to release several seminal horror films over the decade. *The Wolfman* (1941) would even establish the accepted folklore of the werewolf. Universal are still associated with horror – James Wan would work with them for his post-*SAW* project, *Dead Silence* (2007) and the studio released a (widely considered inferior) version of *The Wolfman* in 2010.

Nevertheless, it is instructive to note that horror, in general, exists mainly outside the mainstream, and is generally the province of independent production. *Night of the Living Dead*, *The Blair Witch Project*, *Halloween*, *The Texas Chain Saw Massacre* are all bona fide independent films (that is, not financed or created within the convergent studio system). All of these were successful financially; indeed, all are among the most profitable films released. A film like *The Dark Knight*, with a high expected return on investment (ROI), has a comparatively huge budget, a third of which will be spent just on the film's marketing and promotion. Whereas, at the time of writing, the most profitable film ever is the purely DIY text *Paranormal Activity* (2007), a film with an essential cast of four, one location set, a minimal crew and a deprived marketing budget (relying initially on an active viral campaign). It could conceivably make back its ROI in a single good weekend. *SAW* was financed, according to the producers' DVD commentary, with the producers' own money. Furthermore, deals were negotiated to appease 'talent'. To secure Cary Elwes, the actor was offered a 'points' deal (which subsequently led to the actor suing the studio for unpaid royalties).[8]

The evidence of horror's potential prosperity – with large profit margins, generated by audiences that are seemingly accepting of low-budget films with no expensive stars – may suggest that horror would be an attractive property for the majors. Nonetheless, a glance along the bottom row of your local video store (if such things still exist by the time you read this) will attest that there are hundreds of low-budget shockers that only reach the most niche of audiences, and many more that do not even manage that. It seems that horror hits a mainstream nerve when it presents a *familiar* fear in an *unfamiliar* way, such as in the novel 'found footage' approach of *The Blair Witch Project* retelling the 'lost in the woods' narrative; or the extreme gore codes of *Night of the Living Dead* bringing monsters to vivid life. The studio system, however, operates by securing large profits from *repeated formulas*, only using properties that are speculated to achieve high revenue: it is no surprise that 15 of the top-20-grossing films are sequels. When the major studios do bankroll a horror product, it is usually due to that particular product's pre-sold quality. Paramount's *Friday the 13th* (1980) was developed to cash in on the in-vogue and profitable 'slasher' cycle, which was established by fringe, independent outfits: the film begat eleven sequels before being remade itself in 2009. A *Variety* article about *SAW*'s production company, Lionsgate, suggests that 'the majors, all owned by big media congloms', envy the studio 'for being able to take risks they can't'.[9]

Horror often needs to provoke to be received favorably. On the DVD commentary for *SAW*, a producer talks about its shock value; '[these films] need to scream to get noticed. The bigger and louder the scream, the more people pay attention to you.' Thriving on confrontational innovation means that horror is an unstable quantity, one that is impossible to pre-judge, with audiences responding to it in visceral, unknowable ways: who would have supposed that a home video of a door occasionally slamming open and shut would make so much money (*Paranormal Activity*)? However, the typical low-budget nature of horror means that financial risk is minimised.

The exhibition of independent films is a complex process that usually involves festival screenings and bidding between several smaller distribution studios. This is the route that *Paranormal Activity* and *The Blair Witch Project* took; the makers of the latter even posted pictures of their 'missing' cast around Cannes to raise the film's profile, the film-makers essentially singing for their supper. There are several dedicated horror film festivals that occur annually; the most famous and influential is the fantasy and horror festival in Sitges, Spain, but there is also London's own Frightfest and Scotland's Dead by Dawn. James Wan and Leigh Whannell created their *SAW* short film as a calling card precisely for these types of industry showcases, and it was duly viewed by a Lionsgate 'buyer' who bankrolled the development of the feature film.

A handful of studios are dedicated to the horror genre, and fans recognise these studio brands in the same way that they follow the genre's stars. In the 1950s, the Hammer studio was synonymous with the genre; and, until recently, the Dimension logo (a subsidiary of Miramax, an independent subsequently acquired by Disney) was indicative of a certain type of quality teen horror, such as the *Final Destination* franchise. It is argued that major studios, with their respected investors, are often squeamish when it comes to the macabre content of horror properties: there is a persistent rumor that Screen Gems gave Lionsgate studios *Hostel* (2005) to distribute, as their parent company, Sony, was nervous about the extreme nature of the film.

LIONSGATE

Lionsgate is the smart, surly adolescent of modern American film distribution. Founded in 1995, it is at time of writing (winter 2011), the most successful film distribution company independent of a major in North America. Lionsgate's first box-office success was *American Psycho* in 2000, and its most successful single release was Michael Moore's *Fahrenheit 9/11* (2004). The studio has gained a brand reputation for releasing edgier, less studio-friendly fare. Although Lionsgate won a Best Picture Oscar for *Crash* (2005) the studio is recognised for its genre acumen and related marketing savvy; in short, they understand horror and its audience. This is the studio that released the hardcore horror of *The Devil's Rejects* (2005) and ambiguous paedophile thriller *Hard Candy* (2005) to reasonable success. The studio has acknowledged its genre appeal by grouping horror releases as part of the Fright Club semi-imprint and website. *SAW* was the film that consolidated this aspect, and the franchise is still the studio's biggest commercial success, earning it over half a billion dollars, as of 2008.

MARKETING

SAW's cross-genre appeal as a thriller aside, the film was marketed primarily as a horror text. A lot of horror relies on word-of-mouth to promote its wares, and the genre often finds its true spiritual home on DVD (where the *SAW* sequels outdid the inaugural film's box office). *SAW* was something of a sleeper hit in this respect, and it has also exploited the home entertainment market with differing editions of the same texts – 'extreme' editions and 'director's cuts' of its sequels. The first *SAW* itself has had two separate releases on DVD, an 'uncut' version and a 'special edition', with extra content varying across each release, and each with a slightly differing cut of the film. The extra revenue generated by DVD releases of this kind – extra footage that builds upon the original text, extra features that contribute meaning – cannily exploits the collector/fan mentality and perpetuates the life of a particular text, as does the inevitable re-release on higher definition formats.

These supposedly secondary markets are actually vital to low-budget horror. Often, these genre texts receive limited theatrical release, whereas the home viewing market – taking in DVD rentals/sales, Netflix/LoveFilm video on demand, and television broadcasts – provide second chances for the text to reach its intended audience; and, often, audiences that were perhaps excluded from the theatrical release, as it is easier for an adolescent audience to view such a film as *SAW* at home, than to illicitly enter a cinema. Indeed, in their formative study of the 'video nasty', Kerekes and Slater maintain that, 'the introduction of video into the domestic market was a blessing to the film aficionado … Horror movie fans were those best served, as titles never before seen became available for rent'.[10] Most people's first memories of watching a horror film usually involve forbidden, scratchy VHS, or, increasingly, illicit downloads.

WHAT TYPE OF HORROR FILM IS *SAW*?

To begin to answer this question, we need to locate the text within the wider context of the genre: where is its place within the grander pantheon of horror? Although the fantastic nature of horror clearly has its roots in ancient mythologies and folklore, we see it emerge as a genre proper during the eighteenth century, with the English Gothic tradition. Horace Walpole, the son of the incumbent prime minister, wrote *The Castle of Otranto* in 1764. Regarded as the progenitor of the English Gothic tradition, it is an intricate, sprawling novel that takes as its plot a saga of familial jealousy within the Italian aristocracy, and depicts curses and spectres among its scenarios of torture and dungeons. Within the English Gothic, we read about solitary characters who are preoccupied with death, and exist within sinister, creeping interiors; interiors that are revealing of their protagonist's mental turmoil. An indicative example is the novel by Walpole's prominent successor, Anne Radcliffe. *The Mysteries of Udolpho* (1794) is a gloomy tale involving loss and the imprisonment of its protagonist in a cavernous European castle. Looking at the horror genre's earlier, literary incarnation within the Gothic tradition, we can clearly read a vein of sadistic punishment similar to the cruel intent of *SAW*. In *The Monk* (1796), which is accepted as an important progenitor of the genre, MG Lewis writes '[the flies] darted their stings into his body … inflicted upon him tortures the most exquisite and insupportable'. Critics have suggested that the obdurately complex narratives of the Gothic tradition have precluded successful and faithful adaptations of original texts (although there is the interesting *Otransk_ zámek*, 1973–4, Jan Švankmajer's 15-minute take on the *The Castle of Otranto*). The horror genre would mutate into more streamlined, gorier cinema texts only towards the end of the century; the Gothic tradition's grist is physical and mental anguish, augmented by dark, shadowy interiors. The links to *SAW*'s merciless concerns of suffering and body horrors are abundantly clear within these early, blueprint texts, proving that *SAW*'s concerns are entrenched within the genre's earliest musings and placing Wan's film within an enduring canon of misery.

Following the progress of horror's pulsing vein, we can next trace *SAW*'s *mise-en-scène* of claustrophobia and sadistic intent to Edgar Allen Poe. Alongside HP Lovecraft and Arthur Machen, Poe is perhaps the most influential of all post-eighteenth century horror authors, whose work did much to cement the iconography and atmosphere of the modern horror film. It is unsurprising that his stories have been filmed by a 'who's who' of horror auteurs, including Roger Corman, Jan Švankmajer, Dario Argento and George A Romero. Poe's work is intensely cinematic; using lexical sets of chiaroscuro lit night and shadow, establishing vivid realised scenes with deliberate and varied use of concrete nouns, and telling stories in macabre first-person voiceover. The parallels between *SAW* and Poe's narratives are especially perceptible. As in *SAW*, Poe's protagonists are usually trapped within psychological/corporeal traps of their own making, and, unlike English Gothic, these characters, just like the cast of *SAW*, are almost exclusively male. In *The Black Cat* (1843), the central character has murdered an old man who has a strange eye, and suffered the fatal repercussions of remorse. Another has been found guilty of an unexplained crime by the inquisition, and left to die in an elaborate chamber of punishment; 'I could no longer doubt the doom prepared for me by monkish ingenuity in torture', (*The Pit and the Pendulum* [1842] a story that features maybe the most famous torture trap in literature, and which was explicitly referenced by the *SAW* franchise in *SAW V*). Akin to *SAW*, Poe's narrative writing is driven to demonstrate corresponding sequences of decadence and punishment, which play out in restrictive, deadly settings. The filter-lit, subterranean levels of *SAW*'s warehouses are pre-dated by the garish hues and gory punishments of Prospero's castle in *The Masque of the Red Death* (1839) and in the crumbling interiors of *The Fall of the House of Usher* (1842). Poe's 'gothic entombments' are reductive, 'shutting down the American frontier' and 'repealing the idea of progress';[11] while other American literature of the period was concerned with the concept of development or 'the quest' (most conspicuously, Melville's *Moby Dick* [1851]), Poe turns his gaze inwards. *SAW*'s DNA consists of this particular tradition of American horror, an insular convention that trades on psychological terror and corporeal punishment, ritualistically enacted in basements and secret rooms.

'TORTURE PORN'

Although its two major forebears in terms of cinematic narrative are the films *Se7en* (1995) and *The Cube* (1997), *SAW* is the film heralded with founding the 'torture porn' cycle. *Hostel* (2005) was actually the first film to receive the lascivious epithet, coined by the *New York Magazine* film critic David Edelstein,[12] but it is arguable that *SAW*, with its immense popularity, did more to consolidate the term and subgenre within the public imagination. 'Torture porn' refers to a subgenre of horror film that focuses in extensive, graphic detail on the infliction of pain and suffering. Following *SAW*, torture porn became so ubiquitous that even art-house directors appropriated its concerns; witness the in-jokery of Lars Von Triers *Anti-Christ* (2009), and, indeed, the watch-it-if-you-can-bear-to *The Passion of the Christ* (2004). It is worth mentioning here, also, the horror curio *Kolobos* (2004), which pre-dates *SAW* by four years. *Kolobos* is an early attempt to incorporate reality television within a wider horror framework: wannabe '*Big Brother*' style housemates fall foul of a house rigged with torturous booby traps. If this film was not a direct influence on *SAW*, then it is at least indicative of the horror zeitgeist circa the early 2000s; spectacles of pain and suffering, within enclosed, inescapable settings (the anxieties of Poe resurfacing au debut de siècle).

The lurid sobriquet 'torture porn' is curious, as the compound phrase would seem to promise an explicitly sexual, or at least titillating, outcome within the films, which is not the case. A film about privileged male American backpackers touring and sexing their way across Europe, *Hostel* does contain sexual content. But it does so in order to illustrate the film's moral stance concerning power and abuse, with the movie's narrative (rather heavy handedly) alternating the sexual exploiteering of its protagonists in the first half of the film with their gruesome come-uppance in the second half. True, a minor entry within the canon, Roland Joffe's *Captivity* (2007), uses the glossy appeal of Elisha Cuthbert as a USP; but, essentially, *SAW* features no scenes of a sexual nature. This is unusual for horror, where sex and death are often closely aligned; for thematic purposes from an artistic perspective, but also for the commercial potentials of exploitation.

In this sense, torture porn remains true to Poe, where eroticism is transferred to convulsions of horror. The cycle substitutes sex with power; penetration with sharp objects are its physical infiltrations, blood the primary bodily fluid. Therefore, the movement's umbrella term refers to the *display* of suffering, the spectacle of bodily trauma – and whatever complex gratifications this exhibition involves. This principle has little to do with being 'scared' or 'creeped out', but is yet consistent with audiences' taboo, eternal fascination with the bloody mysteries of its own mortality. Death and gore have been displayed and commoditised for centuries: witness the Victorian galleries that towered around medical operations, or the public hangings, both swollen with paying, public attendees. SAW is a continuation of this principle at its most direct; a spectacle of suffering that allows audiences to explore notions of their own humanity and its limits from a safe, responsible distance (responsible as, after all, no one is *really* being hurt or killed within horror's artificial diegesis).

The Victorian era was in fact a seminal age where horror is concerned. Between 1837 and 1901, many archetypes and tropes of the genre were consolidated and popularised. Dracula and Mr Hyde stalked the pages of late-nineteenth century literature, séances captured the public imagination and Jack the Ripper served up real-life horror to an emerging news media. Theatre produced some interesting scenes, also: in Paris at this time, Oscar Méténier was preparing his *grand guignol* puppet show. Translated literally, *grand guignol* means 'big puppet show', but the phrase has since become synonymous with a particular brand of gory spectacle. It was also an ironic comment on the intimacy of the room where the show was performed; a small space wherein packed audiences were intimately confronted by the dramatic spectacle. Originally, the stage exhibited naturalistic fare, but the theatre soon became well known for the shocking experience of its horror plays. Titles such as *L'Horrible Passion* and *Le Laboratoire des Hallucinations* became crowd-pleasing dramas, wherein rape and murder narratives would occur. The *grand guignol* stage was a theatre of cruelty, where primitive special effects depicted torn flesh, acid burns and eyes being ripped out, all staged within the close settings of the tiny stage. Guignol, the Punch-like archetype and main recurring character of the plays, was a mischievous trouble-maker, and would usually end the puppet show by being punished in a most unpleasantly visceral fashion for the gratification of the baying audience. Reportedly, the puppeteers would throw out actual animal meat and blood during the hardcore pantomime climaxes of these shows, which were adaptations of stories from well-known writers, the most fitting example being Edgar Allen Poe. Billy, Jigsaw's puppeteer avatar, seems to be a resurrection of Guignol: impishly presiding over scenes of gore-washed sadism.

The impish Guignol puppet of Parisian theatre

Grand guignol is arguably the earliest visual representation of gory codes and conventions that would become *SAW*'s raison d'être. Early cinema horror eschewed this type of visceral imagery, however. The Universal horror cycle of the 1930s essayed texts of atmosphere and the uncanny, but it was only during the sixties (with the development of colour technology) that blood began to liberally splash the screen. Alan Jones asserts that with 1963's *Blood Feast*, Herschell Gordon Lewis 'was responsible for the forerunner of the splatter genre, with a film that updated *grand guignol* trickery with its mutilation shots';[13] and there was also the monochrome cannibalism of *Night of the Living Dead* in 1968. Narratively, however, the obvious precedents to the torture porn genre are the seventies 'Rape and Revenge' films, in particular Meir Zarchi's *I Spit on your Grave* (1978), recently remade to capitalise on the current vogue for gory revenge dramas. Within the 'Rape and Revenge' cycle, we see *SAW*'s unforgiving Old Testament morality already being acted out in unflinching, primeval detail: first the miserable sexual abuse, then the celebratory revenge; an eye for an eye, rape begets castration. In a manner similar to *SAW*'s righteous castigations, the viewing 'pleasure' lies within witnessing the comeuppance of moral deviance.

Eighties horror was dominated by the 'Stalk and Slash' cycle, where the dominant motif is pursuit, a chase that is eventually truncated with a fatal blow from the killer: think of Sally jumping from the window in *The Texas Chain Saw Massacre*, Nancy slipping in dreamy blood in *A Nightmare on Elm Street* (1984). The slasher cycle lives on in modern cinema in the form of the 'Urbanoia' film, wherein a 'group … are hunted down and are killed'.[14] In *The Descent* (2005), the all-female troupe play cat and mouse with the subterranean mutants, as does poor Kate (Franke Potente) in *Creep* (2004). In contrast to these films' conspicuous use of space, the recurring sequence of torture porn is repression and claustrophobia, as if the fleeing suburban kids of the Eighties 'slasher' films grew up to an adulthood of incarceration. In *SAW*, victims wake to find themselves pinioned to the torture device; *Hostel* provides a similar scenario; as does *Captivity*, from its title onward. The antagonists of torture porn are not as sporting as their masked predecessors, capturing their prey with the use of soporific drugs and not giving them even the merest chance of escape. There is rarely a sense of 'the chase' in these latter films; victims are held static, save for the spasmodic twitches their restraints will allow. Here, anxiety is caused by isolation and inescapable confinement. Modern horror has internalised its unease again. Its concern is the self; how far can its cinematic excesses go, and how much can the audience withstand?

In terms of *SAW* and its sequels, the representation of this anxiety is double edged, with both aspects working on the principle of a cumulative dynamic; diegetically, how much pain can the protagonist weather to survive; and, non-diegetically, with how much of the spectacle of atrocity can the audience cope? Each sequel attempts to 'one up' the previous film in terms of cringeworthy violence, almost childishly challenging the viewer to watch. The tagline to *SAW II* is, 'We DARE you again'. For the horror fan, this boundary pushing is a major pleasure (a friend gave up after *SAW III*'s 'hog bath'; therein was his threshold). The challenge has always been at the forefront of the genre's marketing minds; a poster for a Universal double bill of the original *Dracula* and *Frankenstein* dares audiences some seventy years before *SAW*, and exploitation flicks of the 1950s offered promotional sick bags to audiences. Lionsgate's marketing department must have been overjoyed when the BBC reported the money-can't-buy publicity garnering headline of 'Film fans faint at *SAW III* show', and the subsequent story detailing how 'staff at a UK cinema have had to call emergency services three times in one night because of a spate of people passing out' during the film.[15] Indeed, the horror auteur William Castle would actually employ shills to faint during performances of his

American poster advertising Dracula *and* Frankenstein *circa 1938*

gimmicky masterpieces. In demographic terms, the horror fan is the adolescent male; the provocative nature of horror marketing taps into this audience's inherent need to 'prove oneself'. For them, the horror film is a comparatively 'safe' rite of passage. It is tempting to imagine this audience identifying with the bluff macho posturing of Adam and Dr Gordon, and aspiring to their ultimate catharsis.

GENRE AND HYBRIDITY

Clearly, SAW is of the horror genre. Its *mise-en-scène* transmits the requisite sense of alienation and disgust, while its principle characters fulfil the dichotomy of killer/victims. Themes of terror and scenes with gruesome content dominate the film, and later we will see how the film was marketed squarely as a horror.

However, what is perhaps most interesting about the generic patterning of SAW is its debt to the crime and thriller genre, or the *giallo* film – an Italian crime horror genre that is notable for its expressive use of lighting and music, and outrageously violent set pieces. SAW is foremost a mystery, built upon a narrative enigma; why are the men trapped and who has trapped them? The cumulative build of the narrative often invites us to guess at this key aspect of the plot. We know that the killer has chosen Adam and Gordon for a specific reason, hence the detail of his plan, but *not* what that reason is. This type of teasing ambiguity is integral to the thriller. Throughout the film, we see and hear the typical crime iconography of police stations; uniforms, hackneyed dialogue, guns. The film's muted colour scheme is reminiscent of crime, too. *Film noir* used key-lit monochrome to exemplify its ethical universe of black, white and grey: the

Detective Sing (Ken Leung) scours the crime scene

good, the bad, and the murky moral grey area between. *SAW* is a *psycho-noir*; the horror film appropriating the two-toned lighting codes of the Fifties crime thriller in its juicy interplay of glowing colour and darkness.

The appropriation of crime tropes invites us to question the film's plot points, as we would a thriller. Audiences can treat the first *SAW* film as a mystery of sorts; and, in this sense, the film provides an extra, grimy layer of narrative pleasures on top of its solid horror gratifications. As the plot progresses, we actively look for clues within the narrative (which *are* there; we see Tobin Bell in a hospital bed, for instance, and, closer inspection pleasingly reveals he is designing some sort of device in a sketchbook). Part of the reason that the reveal of Jigsaw in the film's climax works so well is because it is tenuously possible to guess it before the film's outcome.

This aspect of the film's narrative – the clues, the intricate causal narrative – has been built upon and extended throughout the *SAW* series. The technique involves fans on a cerebral level, and an active one too; forums pore over lines of dialogue and seemingly throwaway scenes, searching for significance. The return of Dr Gordon in *SAW 3D* is a deliberately fan-pleasing manoeuvre, having been mooted for years on *SAW* message boards (listening to the commentaries on the *SAW* DVDs, one is struck by how much reference is made to fan boards by the producers of the texts; it is clear that they are conscious of this hardcore aspect of their fan-base).

At the time of writing, a forthcoming project of Leigh Whannell and James Wan's is purported to be an explicitly *film noir*-style crime narrative. This is a natural development, as *SAW* contains enough tropes of the crime genre to be comfortably considered a hybrid of horror and thriller. Whannell states on the commentary for *SAW III* that 'Originally, James [Wan] intended [*SAW*] to be a Hitchcockian slow burner, a very studied thriller, like *The Usual Suspects* (1995)'.[16] While it is not an original process for horror to be influenced by The Master – countless slashers have aped the confused sexuality and weapon of choice of Norman Bates, and *The Birds* (1963) is the clear forbear of apocalyptic horror – *SAW* homages *Rear Window* (1958) in Adam's flash-lit stumble through his darkened apartment. The Hitchcockian resources that are drawn upon pertain to mystery and suspense.

While the *SAW* films that followed the original have dampened this approach, the narrative of the original *SAW* certainly piques our inner detective: we are witness to duplicitous plotting, mystery and red herrings. Who is behind these mysterious machinations, these complex killings? When the film's devastating twist is executed, it is a crime-like reveal – 'hedunnit'. Jigsaw stands up, dominating Adam; even, rather unnecessarily, giving him an extra shock for good measure. We are given a montage at this point, a technique that will become de rigueur throughout the series, reviewing pertinent plot sequences at whip speed, encouraging us to admire the ingenuity of the plot structure (a crime trope that reaches way back to Poe again, with the *Murders in the Rue Morgue* [1841]).

The script draws on the crime genre to populate its film in terms of its characters, too, appropriating many stock archetypes, and the situations they interact within, from the *noir* tradition. There is the morally suspect Detective, the seedy photographer, the icy blonde; there are affairs and procedural details, and for the most part, the deaths are treated as murders, rather than the disposable deaths typical of horror films. In the genre, a killing usually marks the end of that character's narrative arc: the investigation of the murder takes place outside of the film's narrative. In *SAW*, this procedure is essential to the film's plot. In terms of the film's locale, *SAW*'s sets take in the crime milieus of police stations and warehouses. There is even a car chase, which, by a happy accident due to the film's low budget, is shot in the rudimentary style of a Fifties thriller, with the 'PMP' ('poor man's process') of shaking the car and lighting to imply movement.

These generic accoutrements are partly continued during *SAW II*, but are increasingly jettisoned throughout the series, all but gone by the advent of the sixth episode (the seventh film does feature a rampage that takes place in a police station, but this location is used and lit explicitly as a horror set, not as a procedural trope). But in the first *SAW*, these generic trappings are more than window dressing (that is to say, tropes that don't serve any more meaningful function than supporting the horror). They are signifiers that create meaning and connote further layers of interpretation. The crime features are a rigid context that the chaos of horror can thrive within, like the dark swirling shades on Hieronymous Bosch's rigid frame,[17] providing the film with much of its narrative drive.

FOOTNOTES

7. Kermode in Barker and Petley, 1997: 57–66
8. www.joblo.com/horror-movies/news/elwes-sues-saw
9. www.variety.com/article/VR1117942674?refcatid=13&printerfriendly=true
10. Kerekes and Slater, 2000: 63
11. Paglia, 1992: 572–579
12. www.nymag.com/movies/features/15622/
13. Jones, 2005: 36
14. Rose, 2009: 13
15. www.news.bbc.co.uk/2/hi/6101704.stm
16. Whannell, SAW III DVD commentary, 2007
17. Hieronymus Bosch (1450–1516) was a Dutch Painter noted for his 'Hellscapes': detailed and vivid depictions of the underworld and the pain and suffering that constituted that realm (see 'Christ in Limbo' or 'Hell' for two especially arresting examples). His paintings were nightmare images, yet, like SAW, Bosch's vision illustrated moral and spiritual concepts.

TEXTUAL ANALYSIS

To begin a closer study of *SAW*, it is prudent to look in detail at its opening sequence. *SAW* is a film that is committed to economy and contraction, from its imprisoning *mise-en-scène* to its narrative organisation. Within the opening sequence the film's theme and what are established with a typically vicious efficiency (all textual discussions of the film use the *SAW Special Edition* DVD cut).

SAW opens with the disorientating close-up of a face under water. An electric blue light on a key chain is the only source of illumination, and, as the chain slowly descends through the water, its glow cuts through the murk to illuminate a man's closed eyes and shut mouth. The intertitles share the same powdery hue as the water, and they too shimmer and waver as if sunken, blurring the diegesis. With abrupt shock, the face – its eyes and mouth – opens with an audible gasp. There follows a montage of close-ups: the water's oily surface tension rippling; the face convulsing; and what looks like a plughole. The confusing haste of the edit, along with the impenetrable *mise-en-scène* and the tight angles, serve to obscure meaning. The audience are disorientated immediately. We cut to a medium shot; it transpires that the face is submerged within a filthy bath.

In this opening minute, *SAW* has neatly presented its thematic interests, and positioned its audience, with the narrative efficiency that is characteristic of this slick, clever film. While most horror films are absorbed by presenting new and different ways to suffer and die, *SAW* is concerned with different ways to suffer and *live*; the trajectory of repression to emancipation, water to air, is indicative of the narrative to follow. The film encourages an intense identification with its 'protagonists', smudging the boundary between dank torture chamber and dark cinema auditorium.

We see the character of Adam, the first victim, stagger and cough; the space that he is within is dark and unfamiliar. The film has already subverted narrative expectations by dispensing with an establishing shot, so we the audience are likewise alienated. The whoosh of running water fills the surround sound of the mix, and the first spoken words of the *SAW* franchise are, 'Help! Someone help me!' This phrase will become the series' linguistic leitmotif, echoed by tens of hapless victims. The use of light is highly manipulative in this opening sequence; when Dr Gordon (we do not see Cary Elwes' character initially, only hear him, encouraging our bond with Adam) finds the light switch, the florescent strip lighting is a sharp, retina-shrinking blue, coruscating to the audience whose eyes have become accustomed to the film's tenebrous opening. A boom sounds with the illumination of each light. Like Adam, we recoil. Our identification is fortified by the inclusion of several point-of-view shots from both characters; some of these are even blurred as their eyesight adjusts to their surroundings.

The characters jolt and wrangle their chains, but they may as well be static, so pinioned are they to the grimy walls of their cell. Conversely, the camera is carefree, darting about the cell, soaring above a motionless body, and finally dive-bombing it in a twisting, corkscrew zoom. The camera's strutting manipulation of space seems to mock Adam and Gordon's entrapment, and serves to create further unease for the audience.

The pitiless lighting and hard tiles, which are arranged in a rigid square pattern, give the room the immediate connotation of a prison. However, it becomes clear that the location is a bathroom, with the usual accruements of toilet, sink and mirrors. This location has its blackly humorous relevance; in a bathroom we perform necessary bodily functions, some unpleasant, before we can leave. Subliminally, we are reminded of the body's corporeal limitations. In a few moments the audience will have a more abject prompt, when Adam fishes in the blocked toilet bowl for clues ('no solids').

The camera cuts between medium shots of Gordon and Adam, occasionally drawing back to a long shot that emphasises the limited space of the bathroom. When it is filming Adam, the camera is edgy and nervous, jump cutting to close-up and back, zooming in intense stares. Gordon's framing is calmer; the camera remaining static, save for a few gentle pans to follow motion. The angles express character; Adam is young and agitated – 'My name is very fucking confused!' – and he panics as to whether his kidneys have been stolen. Gordon, on the other hand, is collected – 'We need to start thinking about why we are here' – using inclusive pronouns to suggest accord. Gordon speaks in an imperative mode, taking a control over the situation. The screenplay offers the direction that '*it seems that Lawrence, despite being in the situation he's in, is above that kind of uncontrolled reaction. He speaks a bit coldly*'.[18] A clear binary opposition is being established between the two characters.

The lighting is filtered through baby blue hues; a visual clue to the underdeveloped, boyish nature of the protagonists. Adam is seen in a series of defensive poses – crouching, hands aloft, coughing – as if trying to shield himself from the cold illumination. Dr Gordon, a big bear of a man, is nonetheless also shot to emphasise weakness, despite his more impressive physicality; he is backed against the wall, sweat patches darkening his ruffled shirt. After the reveal of the 'corpse', which is positioned between the two prisoners, we see Adam swoon to vomit off-camera: even before the film has begun properly, he is almost defeated! The room is abject, a hostile arena. There is something accusing in its cold, impassive walls, its grime and stink. It is Dante's Third Circle of Hell – 'I see new torments and new souls in pain about me everywhere ... the stinking dirt that festered there' – the resurgent locale of Poe's horror narratives.

The score is a dirge of minor notes; swirling, disembodied resonances and thudding metal percussion. There is an off-kilter air to this music; subtle lacrimosa, rising swells and rapidly descending diminuendos. The staccato percussion, an industrial beat of hollow metal, occurs to underline the significance of clues: the tape recorder, and the cassette.

The sound design attaches significance to certain objects, which are then elevated to the status of 'clues'. The *mise-en-scène* is training the audience to value detail within the iconography, communicating that the film is potentially a mystery of sorts.

In this opening scene, then, *SAW* deftly communicates its themes of entrapment and survival, and establishes its kinetic, distinctive style of horror cinema. It establishes the two characters' situation, their initial attitudes and temperaments and the beginnings of their character arcs. The narrative enigmas and motifs are similarly sown here. Within the linear timeline of SAW, this scene actually occurs at almost the midway point; the film's opening is also its narrative axis.

THE LOOK AND SOUND OF *SAW*

In the Thorpe Park theme park in Surrey, there are two attractions based upon the SAW franchise; a rollercoaster and a 'haunted house'-style maze. The rollercoaster, cutely, takes the form of a 'trap' the riders are stuck within, while the maze involves entering a crime scene and being chased by actors in pig-masks and the like. What is striking about these 'rides' is just how easily transferable the iconography and design of the original film are. The detail of the conceptual design is very thorough: while queuing for the rollercoaster, you are housed in a 'warehouse', and the olive and brown tints, the bloody writing smeared on the walls, is instantly recognisable as the palette of the world of SAW. As the riders sit in the car, the bar descends, and up pops Billy on a screen situated above the tracks to solemnly intone their potential fate; he then makes a physical reappearance at the end of the ride to congratulate us for surviving the ride. Although I am sure that there could be theme-park rides based upon other horror franchises, it is open to question whether the production design of such a ride would enjoy such a successfully recognisable brand identity.

The look of the SAW film is grimily distinctive. In contrast to the gloss that commercial horror often employs, SAW appears grotty and rancid. The glowing textures and the grimy *mise-en-scène* create a world that is hyper-real, yet visually compelling. The roots of the film's look would seem to lie within the gorgeous Italian cinematography of Luciano Tovoli or Gianlorenzo Battaglia; the use of garish filters, the hostility between harsh set illuminations, and clammy, moist key lights is typical of 1980s Italian horror. Critics have noted the similarity between SAW and the *giallo*. Indeed, SAW III's pig bath is directly influenced by the 'flesh pool' in the bizarre *Phenomena* (1985). Further to the film's European influence, in the tradition of the Dutch master, Goya, SAW's day-glo chiaroscuro is expressive of the characters' broken subconscious; tenebrous psychological shadows that suggest shady misdeeds and guilt. The use of light and space within SAW is paramount to its impact.

There is no escape

The film's idiosyncratic style was created by production designer Julie Berghoff and David A Armstrong, the director of photography. Armstrong's career prior to *SAW* was varied but undistinguished, while it was Berghoff's first major film as production designer. Berghoff's work impressed, and she was employed by writer-director Wan for his subsequent features, *Dead Silence* and *Death Sentence* (both 2007). The murky order of *SAW*'s look is consistent in these films. Armstrong has stayed with the *SAW* series as cinematographer; a clear indicator that the visual design of the film is a fundamental element to the series' success.

Space within the film is significant to the film's themes and emotional impact, featuring as it does a series of enclosed spatial areas. Within the first frames we see a key slip down a watery plughole. This begins a collocation of similar spaces; damp and tightened enclosures, either hiding or swallowing secrets. By necessity, all of Jigsaw's chambers make use of confined spaces. Paul's in particular utilises claustrophobia, a room within a room, with the former crammed full of razor wire; the simple instruction Paul is given is to make his way through the space (easier intoned in a gravelly voice than done). Mark's death is within a greasy chamber whose walls hold the combination to open the safe (another space within a space) that holds the antidote. The bathroom where Adam and Gordon are trapped is another such obnoxious arena: as Adam says, 'I went to bed in my shithole apartment, and woke up in an actual shithole'.

The low budget of the film greatly relies on lighting to create the look of the cells, which is certainly distinctive. When Roger Corman made his Poe cycle, he insisted that the films were made entirely on set (the exception is *The Tomb of Ligeia* [1964]) to best express an otherworldly, fantastic feel and retain the author's obsessive claustrophobia. Watching them, even today, there remains a dreamy, hallucinatory beauty within these older texts. However, there is little beauty in *SAW*. Here, light gels and confined spaces give *SAW* its idiosyncratic design and do much to create its oppressive feel, its tight geometries of metal and blood: these sets have ceilings built, which is a deliberate extravagance for a film of this budget. The lighting of *SAW* is often blurred, as if shaded, and often slimy; slick with blood or grease. The edges of the frame often smudge to oblique blackness, which bleeds the film into the dark of the auditorium itself; a non-diegetic, real-world chamber.

Due to the treacherous nature of the traps, the rooms themselves seem powerful and alive. The vivid lighting gives the space rancid vibrancy, an identity. (The only exception to the rule is Amanda's cell, which seems less restricted; Jigsaw's avatar rolls in from the shadows on his trike.) These abysses are feminine in nature, they are wet and the lighting used to film them is filtered as if through flesh. Therefore, the film suggests that the torture chambers are wombs in which the protagonists are reborn – or not. Paul is instructed to move through the tight space, and Mark must open the locked safe to achieve freedom; to achieve rebirth, the uterine seal must be broken. Jigsaw is, in a sense, a parent to his victims; teaching them lessons, offering an extreme 'hands on' school of development. It is possible to read his relationship with his victims as that of a heavy-handed, disciplinarian dad, especially where Amanda is concerned. The idea of Jigsaw as a father is literally explored to poignant effect later in the series, when it is retroactively introduced that his motivation is partly due to losing an unborn child in a senseless accident (which, in a further twist of the screw, turns out to be the fault of Amanda). Like the father of all of horror's mad scientists, Victor Frankenstein, Jigsaw is both father *and* mother to his creations; and, as the series develops, he too will face the wrath of his 'creatures'.

It has been noted that the heavily stylised look of *SAW*, as well as its kinetic edits, has been borrowed from the mid-1990s industrial music scene. The videos of such acts as Ministry and Marilyn Manson share the same grimy shadows as the film, and similar queasy lighting codes. Nine Inch Nails' oeuvre contained several references to pigs, and the video for their 'Happiness in Slavery' showed a man strapped to a torture device and undergoing extreme physical persecution. Horror fans are, stereotypically, fans of metal music and its multitude of subgenres; Rob Zombie of White Zombie has made the transition from heavy metal front man to horror auteur, and more commercial horror films usually have some sort of heavy rock noise on their soundtrack (SAW has Fear Factory's 'Bite the Hand that Feeds' as a synergous extra on its DVD release). This link to the industrial genre of music is made explicit when we consider that the scorer of SAW, Charlie Clouser, was a member of Nine Inch Nails' live band.

SAW's score is composed of incessant white noise; urgent metal throbs, scraping crescendos, empty rises. It is a soundscape that compliments the threatening atmospheres and urban back stages of the SAW universe. Swooping crashes are used to highlight the moments of terrifying recognition that the victims experience, occurring when they realise the potentially fatal aspects of their predicament: the body in the bathroom, Amanda's widening eyes. Incessant hums and whirrs drone at the bottom of the sound mix, reminding us of the film's fretful environment.

The main musical theme of SAW is the incidental score, 'Hello Zepp', a semi-classical piece that uses swelling strings and peaking synths to intense effect. It occurs most notably during the revelatory scene when Adam discovers Zep's tape-recorder, and discerns the plot loops intoned within its magnetic strips. The crescendo is timed to the deep-focus reveal of Jigsaw standing up. The music is mournful, but there is a heroic thrust to the theme, one which supports Jigsaw as a victor. There is also the sense that it is deliberately celebrating the daring narrative twist of the film itself, aggrandising the dazzling plot turn.

Horror themes often pass into the jukebox of popular culture. John Carpenter's Halloween score is iconic, and the theme from The Omen (1976) has become aural shorthand for demonic or mischievous children, most notably as part of a parody in the television sitcom Only Fools and Horses. 'Hello Zepp' is used within all of the subsequent SAW films to communicate the final victories of Jigsaw's creed, and also as part of the marketing campaign (indeed, other films have also borrowed the composition for unrelated trailers). With its iconography of harsh reverberations, the theme locates the film within the horror genre, while its swells and strings empower the narrative, adding grandeur to the film's squalor.

FOOTNOTES

18.   www.imsdb.com/Movie%20Scripts/Saw%20Script.html

Narrative in *SAW*

In horror texts, the narrative trigger for the film has usually occurred several years before the events of the main feature's narrative or plot. In *Friday the 13th*, for instance, Jason has drowned in the Camp Crystal Lake over a decade before the murders begin, and in *Paranormal Activity*, Katie has been haunted since she was eight. In *SAW*, John Kramer was diagnosed with cancer far before the events of the film begins; and we actually see little or nothing concerning his victims' transgressions; we only meet them as they wake up in their traps. What the horror film details is the unpleasant and predestined conclusion of this initial disruption; they depict universes that are tentative and physiologically fractured. Robin Wood would characterise this thematic foundation as 'The Return of the Repressed': 'what is repressed, must always strive to return.'[19]

The innate fracturing by horror of its narrative is part of the genre's assault upon the audience. Tvzetan Todorov suggests that all narratives fall within the structural parameters of *equilibrium* (balance, normality), *disequilibrium* (something disrupts this balance), *new equilibrium* or *resolution* (where the dilemma is resolved). However, this structure is problematic when we attempt to apply it to horror. Just as the disruption is not as much 'disruptive' as an inevitable aspect of the film's narrative line, having been present yet repressed for years, the new equilibrium is fractured and often incomplete. The resolution is rarely reassuring in horror films: as Carrie's hand shoots from the grave (in *Carrie* [1976]), Katie launches Micah towards the audience (*Paranormal Activity*), the audience is not afforded the reassurance of a neat equilibrium. When *SAW* ends, Jigsaw walks away and intones, 'Game over', but while his sport may well be at a conclusion, the climax leaves many threads. Gordon is presumably fatally wounded, Adam is trapped; we do not find out what happens to them, and so therefore, the narrative is left unsettled – at least until the sequel, which, when the initial screenplay was written, was in no way guaranteed. Horror leaves its narratives unresolved because fear and anxiety are eternal; it cannot cheat us of this truism, as we instinctively know that this would cancel the genre's impact.

The *SAW* films are especially respected for their narrative ingenuity. The sequential structure of the first film, with its fractured flashbacks and shuffled order, provides a non-linear disorder that mimics the confusion felt by the protagonists. The sequels have continued this tradition, by attempting to expand not only the mythology of the franchise, but the plot of the original film, developing story points and adding detail in ways that allow us to view the first film in new and different ways. In this way, the first film has been given a cinematic immortality; like a werewolf, its savage power is renewed with each fresh cycle. Whannell's spoken desire to make a film akin to *The Usual Suspects* has in a sense been approved; it is possible to re-watch the original film with fresh eyes and insider information, creating a different viewing experience with each new showing.

The organisation of narrative information in *SAW* is one of the film's most idiosyncratic properties. The film employs flashbacks within flashbacks, real-time scenes, sequences that are speeded up, repetition, voiceover and point-of-view sequences. Its manipulation of time is dazzling – more evidence of the intention to disorientate. In the words of Aristotle, 'the most important part is the ordering of the incidents'. *SAW* breaks the fresco of its storyline to pieces, and jigsaws these fragments into fiendish re-order.

Looking at the chronology below, we can chart the linear narrative of the plot and its complex viewing order.

CHRONOLOGY OF EVENTS IN *SAW*

The order of events within the onscreen narrative is indicated by the numbers in brackets.

- John Kramer is diagnosed with cancer (not shown).

- Paul undergoes his trap (2).

- Detectives Kerry, Singh and Trapp create a crime scene in an ongoing investigation (not shown).

- Amanda undergoes her trap (6).

- Mark undergoes his trap (3).

- Gordon meets someone illicitly. Possibly Carla, a medical student (referred to, not shown).

- The crime team investigate the scene and find a torch with the finger prints of Dr Lawrence Gordon. The nickname 'Jigsaw Killer' begins to gain currency (not shown).

- Gordon is treating John Kramer. Zep Hindle is an orderly on the ward (4).

- Tapp interviews Gordon. They both watch Amanda's testimony (5).

- Tapp drives Gordon home, and intimates that Gordon is a suspect (11).

- Tapp becomes increasingly obsessed with the 'Jigsaw Killer'. Following a clue, he discovers Jigsaw's lair. Along with Singh, he saves a man, Jeff, from a prototype trap. However, Jigsaw wounds Tapp, and kills Singh (12).

- Tapp is discharged, and some time later sets up surveillance outside the Gordon house. He commissions Adam to photograph Gordon (10).

- Diana Gordon wakes up afraid in the Gordon house. Gordon comforts her, but leaves (7).

- Zep invades the house, kidnapping Alison and Diana (8).

- Gordon meets Carla (17).

- Upon leaving, he is photographed by Adam (15).

- Gordon is abducted (13).

- Adam is abducted at home (14).

- Adam and Gordon awake in the bathroom (1).

- Zep continues to terrorise Diana and Alison (9).

- After tribulations in the bathroom, Gordon receives a call from Alison (16).

- In the Gordon household, there are struggles, and shots are fired (17).

- Tapp rescues the women, and chases Zep to the warehouse (18).

- Gordon cracks and saws off his leg, as Zep struggles with Tapp somewhere in the warehouse. Tapp dies (19).

- Zep bursts in, and Adam kills him (20).

- Gordon crawls off (21).

- Jigsaw rises. Adam is left to die (22).

The intricate narrative structure of SAW is a vital aspect of the film's location of audience. The audience themselves are invited to 'play a game', to make sense of clues, to synthesise the non-linear progression into sense. Of course, we rely on our genre knowledge to navigate these intricate plot mechanisms; we know that there is a threat (there is a 'dead body' within the film's opening moments), and that the protagonists must overcome this threat. Claude Lévi-Strauss theorised that all narratives work on the principle of 'binary opposition', the ongoing creation of conflict/opposition. These oppositions can be visual (light/dark), or conceptual; in the case of SAW, subjugation/freedom. In SAW, our understanding of Lévi-Strauss is a narrative touchstone; in the unreliable, trapdoor story with its narrative tricks, the only sure thing is the danger the protagonists find themselves in, and their dire need to escape.

An example of a trick that SAW plays on the audience regards the eventual reveal of Jigsaw's identity. Throughout the film, by way of an overt series of red herrings, we are led to believe that it is the weasely Zep who is behind the Jigsaw campaign. We first see him spying on Gordon and Adam, and as the narrative progresses, the audience are given more information about Zep, his job and his thoughts (he's a 'very interesting character', he says about John Kramer). He is centralised by the film; we have close-ups of him, and the information we receive following his 'reveal' as the killer serves to consolidate him as an antagonist (*Aha! He is linked to Gordon as they both work in the hospital – of course, it was him all along!*). When we see him taunt poor Diana and Alison, our inner juries are convinced … he is a bad and cruel man. We have found our Jigsaw. However, this is another of the true Jigsaw's ruses, a final game that is played not with the characters, but with the *audience*. As we leave the cinema, the film lives on; we question what we see and replay events, providing our own flashbacks from memory to explain the film's narrative.

SAW's narrative is multifarious, turning in on itself as the film plays out, causing whoever is watching to further question what they see. We are privy to flashbacks, repeated sequences, flash forwards, bridging voiceovers. The timeline is tied deliberately tight like one of Jigsaw's knots, and the audience is invited to involve themselves in extricating themselves from the curious puzzle. Perhaps the only element that seems placeable is the warehouse where Dr Gordon and Adam are trapped; it is the film's central location, and within its confines the camera is often static, its shots longer, and this strengthens our identification with the two characters. Psychologically, the audience are as steadfastly located here as Adam and Dr Gordon.

FOOTNOTES

19. Wood in Jancovich, 2002: 27

REPRESENTATION

WOMEN IN *SAW*

Horror literature and films have been the source of much academic consideration regarding gender representation. Poe famously claimed that 'the death of a beautiful woman is the most poetical topic in the world',[20] and horror has, traditionally, followed this credo, wherein the dominant form involves male killers stalking female victims. However, to reduce the horror film to an entirely misogynist genre would be a simplistic appraisal, and would be to overlook the pantheon of strong female characters that continually triumph over phallocentric evil. It is also a view that would dismiss the psychosexual anxieties that drive the genre, anxieties that are clearly explored within the first *SAW* film.

As the *SAW* series progresses, the character of Amanda, played by Shawnee Smith, increases in significance within the overarching narrative and she becomes an icon. In the first film, her screen time is limited to just two cross-cut scenes. Nonetheless, these scenes – one visceral, the other harrowing – are standout sequences within the narrative, and are crucial to the film's ideology.

We first view Amanda from a specifically male point of view. Through a windowed wall, Gordon watches from an adjoining office as she is being escorted into the police interview room. A large man, guiding her with his hands on her shoulders, shadows her and in turn is followed closely by Detective Tapp. Amanda cuts a vulnerable figure, her gait is tentative, and we do not at first get a full impression of her face; she looks down, and shuts her eyes in a close-up cut. She wears unfussy black, and her hair is greased back into a ponytail; there are no scopophiliac male pleasures to be gained here. The audience are further barriered from her by the hefty desk that she sits behind.

Her only concession to any sort of accessory is the laminate visitor's pass which is pinned to her chest; white with an outsize crimson 'V' dominating. The film magazine *Sight and Sound* intertextually linked this scene to Alan Moore's comic book series *V for Vendetta*, which is also about a moral zealot whose unorthodox, extreme torture techniques transform the spiritual outlook of a young girl he has imprisoned.[21]

Amanda (Shawnee Smith) sees that there is no easy way out

Amanda is introduced to Gordon as the victim who managed to escape, defining the character for audiences in terms of her survival. In the confined male landscape of *SAW*'s world, it is significant that 'the only one who made it' is female; and also perhaps important that she had to conquer another male victim to survive. Significantly, no female character dies in *SAW*, compared to the confirmed five, possibly seven, male deaths: a ratio that is in sharp contrast to typical horror body counts.

In flashback we cut to Amanda's ordeal. Her trap is, as Jigsaw helpfully explains in his bespoke video, 'a bear trap in reverse'; she is tied to a chair, with a heavy iron contraption barred across her mouth and head. The idea is that the trap is sprung upon on a timer; after so many seconds, it will snap shut, crushing her head unless she can retrieve the key to unlock it. Trickily however, the key is hidden in the stomach of another of Jigsaw's casualties, an unidentified male who is drugged and asleep in the chamber.

It is easy to understand why Shawnee Smith was cast in the part of Amanda. The severe architecture of her face – glacial cheekbones and deep, whirlpool eyes – essay fear with superlative effect. Smith's eyes are ringed with thick kohl to heighten expression, and it is a shame that the film reverts to the rapid whip pans and frantic speed lapse to express Amanda's terror as she escapes the chair, as Smith's trapped animal stare would have been horribly sufficient in itself. The crazed montage of panic will become a hallmark of SAW's style, though, serving to complicate the audience's reception of the trap: an identification/voyeurism dichotomy.

Amanda, however, does not fall prey to her terror; she struggles fiercely and the ties soon snap. The camera relaxes to a sequence of medium dutch angles as Amanda breaks free of the chair and stands above her cellmate's body. It is intriguing how she does not attempt to 'escape' the cell at this point. She does not look for an exit, a broken window or door. Instead, we see her tentatively walking toward the victim. Previously, we have seen male victims freak out and panic, ruining any hope of escape. But in Amanda's case, as she has escaped the chair ties, we have already seen a minor triumph from her; and she now seems emboldened. She is frightened, but she is also sure; she knows what she must do. Escape is not an option. As Jigsaw entreats her to 'live or die, make your choice', the camera slows to emphasise Amanda's decisive head turn.

Amanda is dressed in an 'emo-uniform' of fishnet stockings, calligraphic tattoos, and long sleeves (the significance of which will be realised later in the sequel). This outfit serves as camouflage: it is iconic of SAW's dark *mise-en-scène* and Amanda is of this world. Atypical of female representation in horror, the dress codes obfuscate Amanda; her body is not 'on display'. As always, the focus is on identification, not objectification. Although, in effect, she is 'rescued' by Jigsaw, Amanda is no Proppian Princess;[22] she is actually the film's sole 'hero' as she completes a journey that irrevocably alters her, executing a sacrifice as part of her trajectory. This narrative sequence *does* rely upon a classic Todorovian structure: Amanda's hedonistic half-equilibrium; the disruption of entrapment; the struggle toward a gory resolution and an improved, wiser Amanda – a new equilibrium. Within the diegesis, there is an extra level of perceived control, as Amanda tells her own story via voiceover: 'And then I saw the body.'

The sequence that follows is especially brutal; it was, in fact, the sequence that Whannell and Wan shot as their initial calling card, although the short film features Whannell in the 'Amanda' role (can we assume that the character's eventual gender change is significant?). The key to the reverse bear trap is hidden within the stomach of the sleeping body; to live, Amanda must retrieve the key. As Amanda stabs the unfortunate victim, she is shot from a low-angle, which empowers her; the camera is unflinching in its view, focusing on Amanda in medium shot, then trailing back to the office where she continues the tale, and then straight back; the diegetic squelch of the pen knife carrying across the sequence. The knife is blunt and rather small; it is not a proud phallic substitute, but it is used to violently penetrate in a series of thrusting stabs. In true *Psycho* style, we do not see the knife entering; our focal point is Amanda, a series of medium angles that illustrate the harrowing effects of her actions upon her face. In what must be this film's goriest sequence we see Amanda sort through entrails that are the bright red of child's paint; Herschel Gordon Lewis gore[23] that emphasises the abject terror. Another horror trope is evident before the stabbing starts; a silhouette of Amanda's hands and the knife raised – her empowered 'double', a dark, powerful reflection of the person she will become.

In a series of jump-cuts, and close-ups of slippery, bloody fingers and rusty locks, the device around her head is removed, clatters to the floor and springs into fatal action. The new Amanda is revealed.

The sound most associated with women in horror films is the scream (indeed, in the film-within-a-film of De Palma's *Blow Out* [1981], 'Co-Ed Frenzy', all that is called for from the girls auditioning for the role of the victim is 'tits and a scream'), but we hear no such histrionics from Amanda. Initially, of course, she is gagged, but even when the trap is removed, the only noises she makes are the exhausted howls of relief. The Billy doll makes a creepy appearance and informs Amanda that she has won the game. Her escape from the trap has allowed her hair to cascade, and there is a glint of defiance in her eyes as she faces down the Jigsaw toy on his tricycle. It is almost as if the experience has made her more feminine, more powerful, as if she has drawn on a survival instinct that taps the root of her gender.

When we return to Amanda in the interview room, she is humble, downcast. The first thing that Tapp asks her after her harrowing recount is, 'You are, in fact, a drug addict, isn't that right, Mandy?' This present tense assertion is typical of the character's macho impetuosity; he reduces her to her crime. Despite her ordeal, she is still being judged. Tapp is a bully, in direct contrast to Jigsaw, who at least sees the potential for change within us all. In this phallocentric arena of the precinct, Amanda plays her part as sobbing victim; but the final words, as is victory, are hers: 'He helped me.'

In her seminal text, *Men, Women and Chainsaws: Gender in the Modern Horror Film* (1992), Carol Clover outlines the defining feature of 'the final girl' as endurance; she is the character within the horror film who 'did not die: the survivor'. Clover goes on to list the characteristics of 'the final girl' as '[one who] is chased, cornered, wounded; whom we see scream, stagger, fall, rise … she alone looks death in the face, but she alone also finds strength to stay the killer … or to kill him herself'. Amanda is *SAW*'s index of strength, 'the only one who survived'.[24] Whereas the men fail and perish, she triumphs and lives, and her prize is to win back her sense of self. (In subsequent *SAW* films, Amanda goes on to have a greater significance within the unfolding, sequential narrative, becoming Jigsaw's second in command. But within the confines of the original film, she is an important, revealing anomaly.)

Gender representation notwithstanding, it is also important to the film's narrative structure that we see Amanda survive, as *SAW*'s production of suspense relies upon the concept that Adam and Gordon, who are still stuck in the bathroom, *can* escape. It is foregone in horror that there will be a body count. However, Amanda's triumph assures us that Gordon and Adam have a chance. The sequence communicates that Jigsaw does play fair and that there are ways of 'winning' the game. That the eventual ending denies us this prospective 'happy' ending is part of the film's ultimate impact.

Throughout Amanda's sequence, the montage links her and Dr Gordon. A medium-focus shot swaps between the two, playing off Gordon's reaction towards Amanda's experience. Like Amanda, he is static. Detective Sing circles and explains the situation to him; their inert pose echoes their restriction within their torture narratives. As the cops are impassive, Cary Elwes' features are twisted into an overriding depiction of horror; we feel his disgust, and perhaps pity. However, within his final close-up, the camera slowly dollying in, there is a flicker of something else in his face. A gesture that approaches awe: *Would I be able to do what she has done?*

The other female character of significance is Gordon's wife, Alison. Played by Monica Potter, she is in binary opposition to the character of Amanda. With their high cheekbones, they are similar facially, and their characters' names are similarly analogous (three syllables and beginning with the same letter), but Potter's hair is 'sunshine' blonde, contrasted with Amanda's 'midnight' black. This crude signifier is indicative of their roles within the film. Alison is solely defined within 'good girl' female archetypes – mother, wife, victim – while drug addict, subculture Amanda exists on the fringe of accepted morality.

Amanda has an important thematic relevance in *SAW*, while Alison's simple narrative function within the film is to illustrate the flaws in Gordon's character. She berates her husband, telling him that she is 'not sure how much longer she can do this' (referring to the daily grind of their marriage), and seems to echo Jigsaw's *raison d'etre* with her question, 'How can you walk through life pretending that you're happy?' Compared to Amanda, she is rather one dimensional, and could simply be viewed as something of a 'shrew' if she did not vocalise an established theme of the film. Of course, she does show moxie when her protective, maternal instinct is aroused; later, as her accosted daughter Diana calls for her, we see Alison twist into rapid action, her image doubled in the mirror behind (like Amanda and her shadow doppelganger, earlier).

While Alison is no Amanda, the film does suggest that Gordon would have escaped Jigsaw's attentions if he had been a better husband and father. Similarly, it is suggested that Tapp, who, with his threats and unnecessary bluntness, has strayed too far into masculine obsession (it is not merely about solving the case, but 'beating' Jigsaw), and Sing even opines that 'Tapp … maybe you should find a girlfriend'. Tapp fulfils a Captain Ahab archetype: he is alone, obsessed, wounded and driven by an all-encompassing need; indeed, in this sense, he mirrors Jigsaw himself. Through its representation of gender, the film seems to be articulating a conservative, 'family values' ideology; these men require the stability of a comfortable, candid heterosexual unity. As if to underline this point of view, there is not an explicitly gay character throughout the entire *SAW* series (the left-wing journalist and horror film fan, Johann Hari, has teasingly suggested that Billy the puppet even 'looks uncannily like the Tory MP John Redwood').[25] As a side note, the video game of *SAW* continues the narrative of Sing's poor wife, who tries to discover what happened to the detective, extending the male/female dichotomy throughout the series' synergistic offshoots.

The film encourages us to compare and contrast its representations of masculinity. Like Jigsaw and Tapp, Jigsaw and Gordon are also specifically mirrored within the narrative. If we assume that Jigsaw is educated and skilled (taking in his well spoken, considered manner, the imaginative conception and detailed construction of his traps), both he and Gordon are middle-aged professionals. However, Gordon would seem, superficially, to have 'everything' – family, health, prestigious employment; the American dream, no less – and takes them for granted, while John Kramer lacks all of these things. Gordon's occupation is important within the plot structure (it allows him an edge within the survival arena), but the scenes in which we see Gordon at work give us clues to his character. In Carla, Dr Gordon has a student who clearly admires him; this is made plain by a pointed close-up in the scene when we are introduced to Kramer in the hospital. Gordon is more interested in Carla than in his patient, offering her a knowing smile over Kramer's sick bed. The older man takes advantage of the girl's reverence, inviting her to meet at the motel room, presumably for extramarital sex. In the motel, the weird formality of the tryst is underlined by Carla's reference to Gordon as 'Dr Gordon'. Unable to carry through his intention, Gordon calls off the date. Amanda is Jigsaw's student but they enact a different relationship: their association is built on respect – respect for Amanda's life on Jigsaw's part, and gratitude on behalf of the student, who, through Jigsaw, has achieved a kind of salvation.

In Se7en, John Doe ends the film with a self-lacerating monologue, recognising himself as a sinner and bringing about his own destruction. Unlike his more cerebral predecessor, Jigsaw never questions himself, and, as the series develops, he indeed occupies a moral high ground over his clumsier, more hot-headed acolytes, Amanda and Hoffman. While we are not actively encouraged to identify with Jigsaw, there is a clear sense that we are supposed to respect his calm intelligence, and admire his self-motivated salvation (the politics of the individual is another typically right-wing horror trope). The film offers a twisted proof positive of Jigsaw's pedagogy, as Amanda becomes a follower of his bizarre, Old Testament creed: 'He helped me', she admits to the police, as she discusses her ordeal. The thematic relationship between Jigsaw and Amanda, a teacher/pupil, father/daughter antagonistic bond, is explored in subsequent films in the series.

MEN IN *SAW*

Dismembered limbs, a severed head, a hand cut off at the wrist as in a fairytale … all of these have something uncanny about them. As we already know, this kind of uneasiness springs from its proximity to the castration complex.' Freud, *The Uncanny*[26]

The theme of paternity is further investigated in *SAW*'s other male representations, but mainly through Lawrence Gordon. The representation of men in *SAW* acts as a counterpoint to the representation of Amanda, providing deliberate balance to the film's ideas regarding gender. There is the abiding sense that Gordon is imprisoned for his failure to adequately fulfil the basic responsibilities of the expressly male archetype – the husband and father.

Gordon is a father who is neglectful towards his wife and child. He prioritises work over quality time with his daughter, Diana ('with our schedules, its difficult to concentrate on one child'), and cheats on Alice, his wife. Jigsaw places the two women in jeopardy specifically to test Gordon's true feelings for his family.

Whereas Gordon fulfils the absent father archetype, Adam is merely callous. He is a *noir*-ish loner who prowls back alleys in order to photograph others' indiscretions for a living. Within the bathroom, he affects a smart-aleck wit and refers to previous sexual conquests: 'This is the most fun I've had without lubricant.' Bluster is his only defense within this torture chamber. However, his predicament is finally linked to male experience; he admits to Gordon, at the eleventh hour, that he has 'a family too! I don't see them, that's my mistake'.

As a defence mechanism, the two men enact a drama of bravado within the bathroom: 'Just because I'm stuck in this room with you, doesn't mean I have to report to you every ten seconds'; 'Throw me your tape', 'No, you throw me yours.' There is an antagonism that we recognise as understandable mistrust, and a refusal to 'back down', to maintain control; but also, default male arrogance. Adam even clarifies – 'Lets face it; we're both bullshitters.'

It is only when the characters finally put aside this misplaced sense of pride and co-operate that they begin to get anywhere. Gordon has to suffer the ignominy of another man attempting to rescue his family: in their liberation, just as in their everyday lives, he is absent. This is something that he recognises, albeit too late, and which at last spurs him on to perform his eventual, terrible self surgery.

In the cell, Gordon hears Zep's gunshots over his phone. The audience are given the privileged information that his family have escaped, but, as far as Gordon knows, they are still in grave danger. 'My family needs me', he screams, the gunshots spurring him into final, fatalistic action. It is all Adam can do to offer hopeless platitudes ('Calm down': 'There must be a way out of this', etc.) For the most part, the camera is situated on the bathroom floor as it films throughout this sequence, consolidating our identification with Gordon, and also visually expressing the situation: the doctor is at his lowest point.

The scene cross-cuts with Tapp chasing Zep, another sequence that focuses on a male duo struggling for survival. As Zep makes his way to the bathroom, the narrative threads and the various locations of the film are tied together. It is finally time for Gordon to play his game.

Cary Elwes gives a powerful, harrowing performance as he removes his foot with the hacksaw. The performance codes are crucial, as we do not 'see' the actual amputation (just the initial cut); the horror is conveyed through Elwes' dramatics. His screams fill the bathroom, but, as he becomes decisively involved in the task, these screams descend to animal grunts and growls that punctuate his weeping. Adam reacts with understandable panic, his howls contributing to the discord. Gordon takes off his shirt to use as a makeshift tourniquet. The weeping and the removal of clothes are reductive, he is being stripped of pride and dignity, more animal than man, driven by basic survival instincts.

SAW's superb sound design is at its most impressive here. There is the splendidly grotesque squelch and crack of flesh and bone as the tool makes jagged contact (in a sparse close-up), overlaying Adam and Gordon's screams and howls, while the ever-present industrial drone of the score hums underneath. When looking closely at this scene, we can see how much of its abject nature is drawn from this cacophony of terror.

We cross-cut to Tapp and Zep. Tapp's beating of Zep, and Tapp's unlucky death, is contrasted with Gordon's self mutilation. The edits heighten the pace of the film, and communicate the Darwinian ethos of the SAW universe: this is a world where life is a struggle, and only the strongest survive, a world where sacrifice is inevitable. And so, Gordon picks up the gun and shoots Adam. As the film builds to its emotional climax, this 'death' seems most shocking of all, due to the remorseful reaction of Gordon.

Gordon (Cary Elwes) and Adam share a final moment

In the blue wash of the scene, and in the similar dress codes of white tees and denim, Gordon and Adam now even look the same; prisoners in uniform. Zep bursts in –'You're too late!'– with dry ice theatrically emphasising his entry. The amputee Gordon attempts to shuffle towards him, but his actions are limited, as is his expression – 'I'll fucking kill you! You fucking bastard! I'll fucking kill you! I'll fucking kill you!' His profane threats are impotent, hopeless repetitions. Even when he fires the pistol at Zep, the chamber is empty; he's firing blanks. Gordon's actions are recurrent, mechanical; he is driven not by logic, but irrational motion.

Jigsaw (Tobin Bell) is resurrected

It is Adam, however, who reacts effectively. With his shock leap back to life (typical of the genre) he accosts Zep, bowls him to the floor and achieves what Tapp and Gordon could not: he kills Zep. Using the lid of the toilet cistern, he smashes Zep's head in until the ceramic breaks. His actions are again atavistic and fierce; the camera witnesses the brutality from a low angle that accentuates Adam's power. The sequence is cathartic for the audience; it is gratifying to see the captive fighting back, especially against a man who threatens children. Zep is dead, and there are, seemingly, only our two prisoners left.

Adam and Gordon are linked in a close-up, their heads leaning confidentially into one another's. They cry together, and whisper promises – 'You're going to be alright'– with an intimacy that is only possible now that they have 'proved' themselves through demonstrations of their strength and endurance. The entire sequence is filmed in unforgiving, claustrophobic close-up; our position is as inescapable as theirs.

At the end of the film, after both men have made blood sacrifices and collaborated with each other, their relationship is touching; 'I wouldn't lie to you', Gordon finally assures Adam. The dynamic is analogous to the understandings that occur at the resolution of a buddy movie (*The Mismatched Masochists*?). The film emphasises the point by using close-ups of the men's weeping, yelling faces (a contrast to Amanda's graceful acceptance).

The 'space' of the sequence breaks open when Adam finds the cassette player. Flashbacks now shatter the diegesis and twist our understanding of the film so far. The focus fills out to a deeper scope, allowing us to see Jigsaw ascend in the background. Blinking, initially unsteady, with his bald head and gooey smears he is like a baby; and the peeling off of the skull cap is a rebirth motion. Perhaps the games have been not so much a lesson for the victims, as bitter catharsis for John Kramer. Certainly, Adam and Gordon have been broken, unlike Amanda, who, again, drew strength from her encounter, and even expressed gratitude. In the increasing darkness of his terminal condition, Kramer finds illuminative purpose; in association with his obvious sadism, there is an implied masochism in his dedication and own physical suffering (lying prostrate in congealed bodily fluids for hours). Before he can stand proud over Adam, Kramer must also have endured: proving himself and *earning* the privilege.

Within the psycho-sexualised arena of *SAW*, however, escape is only possible when the men abdicate their gender, sacrificing their sexual identity and effectively desexualising themselves. Jigsaw's male victims are invited to shed blood to survive, a symbolic menstruation. Gordon's sawing of his limb is effectively a castration gesture, while Adam, his arm aloft in a parody of the male erection, is left impotent within the bloody chamber when Jigsaw shuts the door on him. Compare this to Amanda's *re*-sexualisation; when she escapes, she becomes stronger, more confident. Is *SAW* suggesting that masculinity, with its arrogance (Gordon) and misplaced sense of importance in the world (Tapp), is in and of itself something that is worthy of punishment?

FOOTNOTES

20. Poe in Thompson (ed.), 2004: 535
21. Osmond in *Sight and Sound* Volume 14 Issue 12, 2004
22. Vladimir Propp (1895–1970) was a Russian critic who, after studying Russian folk tales, developed the theory that all fairy tales narrative feature recurring character types: the Hero, his binary opposite the Villian, the Mentor, etc. The Princess' narrative function was passive: existing simply to be rescued and to provide romantic reward/fulfillment for the Hero. The Proppian archetypes are often applicable to modern texts.
23. Herschell Gordon Lewis (1929–) is an exploitation film maker who earned the sobriquet the 'Godfather of Gore' following splatterfests *Blood Feast* (1961) and *Two Thousand Maniacs* (1963) films that pushed the boundaries of cinematic carnage and visceral horror.
24. Clover, 1993: 35
25. www.johannhari.com/2006/11/03/i-saw-saw-iii-and-survived-
26. Freud, 1919: 243

THEMES AND ISSUES ARISING

POST 9/11 HORROR

It takes a war to release certain emotions, don't you think? Certain impulses to cruelty, kindness, too, perhaps, but anger, rage, injustice, they're all grist to the sadism. Displacement, bereavement, survivor guilt contribute towards providing the victims. And underneath it all, a knowledge of death that makes life more precious to some and more disposable to others. *The Cutting Room*, Louise Welsh[27]

It is arguable that a horror text, when consumed by mass audiences, is indicative of that audience's particular fears or anxieties. Motivated by the zeitgeist, horror mutates and adapts like a virus to society's host, reflecting the varied and contemporary terrors of its era of production. The genre is caught in a continual attempt to keep up, as fictional horror only ever thrives within the shadow of real-life atrocity, guaranteeing the genre infinite material.

The Hammer horror films of the 1950s and '60s were a collection that seized the public imagination so effectively that the studio became a household name. In many ways, these films were period escapism that retreated from post-war society into an opulent, yet treacherous past (un-coincidentally, their antagonists usually had mid-European accents). These too were supplemented, in their turn, by the visceral realism codes of *Night of the Living Dead* and *The Texas Chain Saw Massacre*. This new wave of films located their horror within contemporary America; a society that suffered from the effects of the assassination of President Kennedy and Martin Luther King, and was fractured by the cultural devastation of Vietnam. These real-life events were communicated to America and the rest of the world via the increasingly available medium of television; the Zapruder footage of Kennedy's murder is a real-life horror narrative, and awful footage of mutilation and death was broadcast direct to front rooms from the battlefields of Khe Sanh. New technology had rendered the violence of the modern world (and subsequent history) transparent. In response, horror cinema jettisoned the atavistic symbolism of the vampire and its ilk, along with the gothic and theatrical *mise-en-scène*, to produce narratives that were harrowing in their realism, and unprecedented in their acute use of gore. As a result, horror's 'golden age' was arguably during the new realism of 1970s cinema. This was the decade where films in general enjoyed from a new sense of experimentalism and freedom: Biskind argues that 'it was the last time Hollywood produced a body of risky, high quality work' and that '70s movies retain their power to unsettle'.[28] Horror cinema benefited from radical inventiveness of the era and its contextual zeitgeist of terror and violence.

Following the televised atrocities of September 11 2001, Hollywood institutions were faced with explicitly addressing America's recent anxieties concerning invasion and the country's new-found vulnerability, both of which had seemed impossible before the events of that day. Action cinema saw a resurgence in interest concerning the superhero, who, in films such as *Spider-Man* (2002) or *Superman Returns* (2006), are seen defending American cities (usually New York) from explosive threats, often rescuing victims who are falling from buildings. War films located their narratives within the Middle East; *The Kingdom* (2007) and *Rendition* (2007) are two representative examples of these types of genre texts, which often suggested an element of American responsibility for the ensuing conflict. There is a clearer sense of culpability, of guilt and fear, evident in the horror films that followed 9/11 and the consequent conflicts. The 'War on Terror' is well represented within this genre. The axiom itself is a glib soundbite, shaped for a simplified media impact in a similar manner to the way a horror film tagline is constructed to impress the genre market. The idiom's analogies with horror are further evident; the abstract verb phrase implies a final confrontation with horror's *raison d'etre*: to terrorise. As the genre feeds upon the unease generated by its real-world surroundings, responses to the 'War on Terror' within horror were inevitable. The films produced during this era are telling of America's subconscious reception of the war.

Horror's most expensive retort to the events of 9/11 was Spielberg's remake of *War of the Worlds* (2005), which saw the auteur relocating from his usual suburban milieu to New York and the East Coast (transposing the location from the source material's London), where he essayed a devastating invasion from the point of view of a disparate family. It is still one of Spielberg's harsher films – gone are the chummy extraterrestrials of 1977's *Close Encounters of the Third Kind*, and in their place are carnivorous pillagers. We fear the 'alien invaders', and with good reason. While this Paramount production overwhelmed with its destructive spectacle, other horror reactions were by their nature more intimate. Rather than compile their allusions from the invasive events of

September 11, the most notable of these genre responses represented the American casualties of the consequent war; young, helpless victims of bloody and seemingly ill-motivated acts. Considering the success of this subgenre from another angle, critic Wendy Ide argues that the 'War on Terror' has desensitised audiences: 'with the human capacity for evil demonstrated so unequivocally by 9/11 and its aftermath, the horror genre felt the need to plumb new depths to shock a response out of a jaded audience. Hence the advent of "torture porn" flicks such as the *SAW* franchise.'[29] However, the consistent referential imagery that pertains to the war, and the recurrent themes that are analogous to the senseless misery of that particular conflict may suggest that Ide's argument is simplistic; there is more to horror than sheer spectacle.

Latent slasher films, such as the *Wrong Turn* series, feature young people wandering into territories that they are ill-equipped to deal with, and coming off worse against the hostile locals (the underrated *Wrong Turn 2* [2007] even features an ex-marine who showcases combat techniques as a central character). *Hostel* is a mischievous address of how the rest of the world possibly sees America; arrogant and imperialistic. Eli Roth, *Hostel*'s forthright director, claims that the imagery in the film was inspired by scenes in the Abu Ghraib prison. More patriotic parallels could be located within studio fare. There is a ludicrously thrilling moment in the remake of *The Hills Have Eyes* (2006) – all-American family falls afoul of vicious 'others' in a hot desert landscape – where the protagonist kills a mutant by impaling it with an American flag (as if the mutant, born and raised in the New Mexico desert, was somehow un-American). The film's sequel would consolidate the allusion by having a group of American soldiers take on the monsters.

In a review of one of *SAW*'s sequels, Katy Hayes suggests that the appeal of the subgenre is due to contemporary concerns, asserting that 'we live in *torture-porn times*'.[30] Hayes places the 'effectiveness' of the genre as 'based on the anticipation of pain. Radio, television and newspapers are full of pain'. This further suggests that horror films reflect their particular era, and are symptoms of a wider mood or cultural event. It is impossible to extricate *SAW* from its post-9/11 context. Along with the recurrent images of the torture of impotent victims, the film depicts Americans who are at the mercy of an invasive, resourceful and merciless force, one with its own belief system, a credo that is violently contrary to western decadence and indulgence. The pain and suffering within *SAW* is a savage bricolage of Iraq war atrocity; a montage compiled of Middle America's guilt-sweated nightmares. The torture chambers Jigsaw constructs echo the sadistic extremities of Guantanamo Bay, while the lopped limbs and bloodletting channels the abject and prolific images of hostage executions.

Intriguingly, SAW series producer Mark Burg situates the franchise's horror specifically within American experience: '[Jigsaw's] killing these people who don't appreciate how good they have it in life ... as most people in America don't realise.'[31] In the Gordon household (which is a built set, as are most of the sets in SAW) there is an American flag on the wall. In the police station, there is also an intentionally arranged, de rigueur Stars and Stripes. This iconography would seem to be deliberate: there are no other visual indexical signs within the film, nothing to tell us which city it is, or to tell us which part of the USA we are in; just that this is America. Of course, the cultural signifiers, such as accents and the police uniforms, contribute; further encouraging us to accept that the film is set in America (the film was filmed entirely within a converted warehouse in Los Angeles, although for the auxiliary films production moved to Canada). It is worth noting that SAW was made by two Australian film-makers, and is a representation of America that has been constructed by 'outsiders'; acting as Adam, Leigh Whannell modifies his Antipodean twang to a Californian pitch as the character must be expressly American, likewise the adjustment of Cary Elwes' genteel English accent. While the post-9/11 horror film would never explicitly address its zeitgeist (which would be too crude a manoeuvre for the genre's subtle, allusive nature), the shadow of 9/11 is inescapable.

DOMESTIC INVASION AND THE FRACTURED FAMILY

Mid-twentieth-century horror drew gothic power from the baroque surroundings of Hammer horror castles and stately homes of shady European kingdoms. In contrast, modern horror texts mostly occur within urban locations, or depict domestic settings that are summarily invaded. SAW features both of these modern milieus, and this should further explain where the modern horror genre's ideological concerns lie. Significantly shifting from its dank torture chambers and subterranean lairs midway through the narrative, SAW makes a point of depicting terror bleeding into the ostensibly safe environment of the American home, and shattering the illusion of familial and domestic security therein. As part of his game, Gordon's family are kidnapped and held to a ransom of sorts; can Gordon deliver, or will they die?

The screenplay explicitly suggests that the Gordons' living room should be 'definitely the living room of a well-off family'. However, despite Gordon's house having all of the accruements of a successful, middle-class lifestyle – cute daughter, trophy wife, leather suite, luxurious space – the interior of his home is shot to look alienating and oddly synthetic; the opposite of comfortable and 'lived in'. The American dream is achieved, but not appreciated.

The 'real world' sets of SAW– the police station, the Gordons' house – often look flat and artificial. When we see these locations, there are rarely camera shots that emphasise depth of field. We witness Gordon's house in close-ups of furniture, clocks and beds, or from a shallow focus upon the characters. Hard lighting emphasises this style of filming, as does the indifferent iconography. These featureless, bland locations support Jigsaw's credo that the world has lost touch with true, deeply felt sensations.

The 'home' sequence ends with Gordon's wife, Alice, and his daughter Diana, at the mercy of the robed, sadistic Zep. The scene begins with Gordon in captivity, reminiscing ('I've been the thinking of last thing I said to my daughter….'), then, in flashback, Diana wakes up in the dark of the Gordon home. She is alarmed, and seeks reassurance from her father and mother. As she makes her way to her parent's room, her journey is communicated through a series of four dissolves, leaving us uncertain as to the precise geography of the house. The camera kneels to her height, which expresses the child's point of view, and consolidates the feeling of disassociation. Unlike the stark bathroom where Gordon and Adam are trapped, the Gordon homestead is lit with back lights that emphasise reds and create deep, weird shadows; again, what should be familiar is rendered strange and threatening. The recurring motifs of the film are mirrors and clocks – nothing is what it seems, and time is running out. Here, the script specifies 'a strange, mechanical-looking clock' on the Gordons' wall; and Dr Gordon's own desk pointedly features a carriage clock and even a large egg-timer filled with sand. Any shelter or sanctuary within the home is temporary; the ticking clock reminds us that comfort is transient. Even the home, its domestic barriers and its familial constructs, is a scant fortress against mortality. Each second we experience is a second closer to death within the SAW diegesis.

Gordon's clock is in time with the intricate mechanics of Jigsaw's traps

We first see Alison, Gordon's wife, asleep alone in the marital bed, as her daughter, Diana, wakes her to tell her about the man in her closet. Note, though, that Diana goes to her mother and asks her to fetch her father; the film is drawing our attention to the gulf between the parents. Broken homes abound in the horror film. Gordon prioritises his work over Diana and it is clear that Diana is anxious, and fears abandonment. She 'hates' Daddy's beeper, which suggests that the device has interrupted prior family occasions, and she plaintively asks Gordon, 'You're not going to leave us are you?' This fracture within the nuclear family, the threat to family values, is anathema to Jigsaw's staunch moral conservatism. However, there is a sense, as there always is in *SAW*, that Gordon can be redeemed; he sits with his daughter and toys with her toes and makes her giggle. However, Gordon's fate is foreshadowed by his 'little piggie' foot game with Diana, symbolically linking his final punishment with his crime, which is to not be a responsible 'family man'. The pace of the film slows during this sequence; giving Gordon back-story and allowing us to feel closer to the character. However, the 'home sequence' is also important as it represents the film's ideologies concerning familial structures and accountability.

Adam's apartment is a world apart; in fact, it is possible to suggest that the bathroom prison is something of a home from home. It is pared down and functional; the screenplay requires that 'the entire apartment is very rundown, decrepit, dingy and old;

truly a shithole apartment as Adam described it earlier. There is graffiti on the door and walls, the wallpaper is fading and peeling, the refrigerator is dirty'.

Within the narrative, the scene where Adam is kidnapped from his flat occurs close to the sequences that allow our insight into the Gordons' home life. It is significant that we see the living conditions of the characters in order to recognise the democracy of terror; both homes are invaded by hostile forces, any home front is unsafe and conquerable. The juxtaposition is deliberate, as it heightens the relative wealth of the two protagonists, supporting the sub-theme of class and consumption.

Class is an abiding horror theme that is again present in *SAW*. Most of the film's secondary anxieties (after the primary, universal urge to escape, to survive) are located within middle-class, adult experience; domestic invasion, the family. When Kerry plays Paul's tape, Jigsaw even describes him as a 'healthy *middle-class* male' (suggesting that his status in society makes his indiscretions even more unforgivable). The theme of class is underlined by Adam's confession. He tells Gordon that he photographs '*rich guys* like you'. Tapp warns Gordon that he will not escape suspicion just because he lives in an affluent area of the city: 'The sewer lines run under this neighbourhood too, Doctor.' Gordon laments that before he was captured by Jigsaw, his 'whole life was in perfect order'. From *Nosferatu* (1922) and *The Cabinet of Dr Caligari* (1920), texts that depicted the aristocratic as villainous, decadent overlords who exploited the working-class, to the Urbanoia sub-genre, that at its heart illustrates a fear of subcultures which are usually poor and lacking in civilisation, it is clear that class has provided horror with much of its thematic tension. This is abundantly evident from the Universal era of classic studio horror: Robin Wood notes that 'Frankenstein could have dressed his creature in top hat, white tie and tails, but in fact chose labourer's clothes';[32] the dress codes of the Creature prodding a subconscious class prejudice. In *SAW*, the backdrop of Jigsaw's lairs and torture chambers are abandoned warehouses. Empty and dilapidated, these abandoned spaces are casualties of failed businesses and bankrupt industry, existing only because commerce's reach has outdone its grasp. His victims are fatalities firstly of a corrupt system: a drug addict, a benefit cheat, an arrogant doctor, a voyeur – all symptomatic of a culture typified by greed.

While the film seems to take a jaundiced view of a society propelled by conspicuous consumption and self-centred ideologies, Jigsaw's concerns are more egalitarian. Rich or poor is an irrelevant status, no one is without sin, in his world view. Part of what separates Adam and Dr Gordon is their distance from one another on the social spectrum. Death, however, is the ultimate democracy, and part of SAW's implication of terror is that pain and suffering cannot be bought off with money alone.

And so, Adam is ultimately punished for his adherence to a capitalist ideology, where everything is for sale – even secrets, even privacy. Adam's shifty, criminal nature is revealed in the practiced, slick manner with which he hides the bag of photos and the Polaroid; there is the sense that being deceptive is his default setting. Unlike Gordon, it seems that Adam never really stood a chance at survival, with his key disappearing down an open plughole in the film's opening moments. As established, Jigsaw is not motivated by money but by his strict moral code. While he does utilise technology, it is of an inexpensive, threadbare sort; he is no billionaire Bond villain. Jigsaw's traps give the impression that they are developed and assembled with painstaking handcraft. This serves to consolidate Jigsaw's artisan, self-sufficient position; he is not prey to society's temptations, and does not rely on its structures and hierarchies of privilege. The thorough detail and sick ingenuity of the traps also heighten the horror codes of the film. *What sort of monomaniacal crazy is capable of such focused cruelty?* we wonder, as we take in the organisation of razor wire within Paul's trap, or the convoluted mechanics of Amanda's headwear. The low production values of Jigsaw's traps mirror the 'virtue of necessity' low-budget impact of the best horror films; they are triumphs of grungy creativity, not slick bombast. Writer Marcus Dunstan (SAW IV to SAW 3D) said of the traps that they were actually serviceable mechanisms, 'built to function there on the day … if there's a scalping chair, there really was a chair with working gears to grind and pull your scalp back'.[33] SAW is more effective for its lack of CGI; the traps themselves have an organic, gruesome reality.

The post-millennial tensions provided by the film reproduce the anxieties that tortured America's psyche in the early twenty-first century; questions that concerned materialism, the safety of the home front, and the fear of an invasive, 'other' culture. However, it is typical of horror to relegate such themes to secondary concerns beside the timeless, universal themes of survival and punishment. After all, these are the disquietudes and anxieties that we ourselves repress, relegating these concerns to our unconscious mind – where, in the end, the horror film will always find them.

CONTROL AND FREEDOM – JIGSAW

In *Danse Macabre*, Stephen King's study of the horror genre, the author argues that horror essentially works by eroding our sense of command, as the genre details loss of control. On the macro level, this implies that there are things bigger than our understanding in this world (ghosts, vampires), and that we are simply mortal dust within a wider, unknowable supernatural cosmos. However, within the micro level, horror also serves to show us the restrictions of our bodies and the limits of our supposed mastery of our surroundings. Gordon laments at one point in *SAW* that 'I had everything in order. My life was in perfect order', although this assertion is a mere perception, as, in fact, he was never in control. Jigsaw is the only character with command in *SAW*: all other destinies are subject to his whim. Part of Jigsaw's horror charisma is that he is *always* one step ahead: of his victims, the law, and, most scarily, the audience. Most horror antagonists are unstoppable, until the film's final reel. Jigsaw is not an exception; but his planning, his sadistic organisation and capability, surely adds to any of our awe and fear of him. All that Jason Vorhees, Jigsaw's main rival for cinematic franchise dominance, did in the *Friday the 13th* series was to turn up with a machete and a vindictive attitude. Jigsaw's mode of operation is one of complete power, ensuring that his victims' command is utterly demolished. When discussing *SAW* recently, Leigh Whannel has stated that his film is 'all about control'.

As we have seen, Dr Gordon's character arc involves him moving from a position of authority to one of complete subjugation and remorse. The screenplay offers the direction to Elwes that he should play Gordon in an eminent manner, emphasising his perceived command. During the opening scene, the script reads: 'GORDON: Calm down, just calm down. (*He knows that to remain calm is to remain in control, something he must be no matter what the situation.*)' For male horror film protagonists, control is a barometer of their character; it is when their dominance is diminished that their horror drama commences. One of the most enduring scenes in horror is the explosive 'birth' of the creature from Kane in *Alien* (1979), which grimly details a subversion of the male body politic. Within the torture porn subgenre, *Hostel*'s static male backpackers are subject to other's governance. In *SAW*, the theme of control is developed further in the character of Adam. Part of the thematic conclusion of the film occurs when Adam takes control to 'save' Gordon. Adam reaches up and knocks Zep to the ground, ignominiously beating him to death with a toilet lid. In the final reel, Adam shows decisiveness and selflessness, effectively demonstrating a responsibility to others, and, albeit too late, an amount of control over his own destiny. Contrasting Gordon's degeneracy, Adam expands his character from feckless and panic-struck (a 'strange mix of someone angry and yet apathetic', as the screenplay directs), to a dependable co-operative for Gordon.

Despite his propensity for destroying his victims' sense of control, and demolishing their egos, Jigsaw himself is no agent of chaos. The killer is organised and driven; a contrast to Amanda, Gordon, and Adam, who are flaky and undisciplined (being, respectively, a drug addict, an adulterer and an absentee father). As previously suggested, there is an almost Biblical drive to Jigsaw's reign of misery. Within the tradition of Christianity's Satan, or the Greek Nemesis, he exists within the diegesis of the text in order to reprimand those who have sinned. Jigsaw's theatrical penchant for robes even gives him the appearance of a dark lord. His theatres of punishments are subterranean; dark, moist and humid chambers of hell (the street where the warehouse is located has the referential name of Stygian Street). Amanda is Jigsaw's very own Job, achieving a divine understanding through suffering. Whereas a lot of horror arranges its narratives around chaos overcoming control, Jigsaw is a methodical artisan, a cruel control freak; he imposes sadistic order upon the disorganised, immoral lives of his victims. His mechanisms are feats of dark imagination and superior engineering that are material extensions of his precise, righteous nature (there is an unintentionally hilarious scene in *SAW V* where Jigsaw exhorts the merits of tempered steel). In juxtaposition, the film expresses chaos through the performers' panicked performance codes and the berserk *mise-en-scène*, and, of course, the bloody mess of their post-trap bodies. Order is further present in the gravelled intonations of Jigsaw's instructions, and in the uncompromising, finite tick of the traps' countdowns: life is chaos, in death there is propriety.

Adam completes a transition from negligent to responsible, and he has certainly demonstrated a determined will to live. So it seems somewhat unfair that despite all of this, he still (presumably) perishes. Surely he completed what Jigsaw wanted from him?

Perhaps it is deliberate that in the final scene of SAW, its narrative logic dissolves, and all order is ultimately revealed to be at the mercy of murderous pandemonium and chaos. Even SAW's proposed themes of order and control are unable to withstand the genre's overwhelming gravitational pull.

Nonetheless, for the most part, Jigsaw diverges from other horror antagonists by virtue of his contrary modus operandi; whereas the threat in horror usually wants to kill its victims, Jigsaw wants his prey to *survive*, he wants them to *live*. Live in the purest sense of the word; appreciative and aware of their own mortality. His philosophy is Nietzschian: what doesn't kill them will make his victims stronger and, accordingly, better people. The traps are 'near-life' experiences. This aspect of Jigsaw is a relatively unique sensibility within horror, and has contributed to his status of anti-hero. From his select scenes in SAW, the antagonist has become more important as the franchise has continued; his role within the on-going narrative has been developed and marketing has focused increasingly on various macabre images of Tobin Bell. This is a distinct aspect of a horror antagonist, who is typically afforded leading man status within genre product.

Throughout the first SAW, however, we could be forgiven for not noticing John Kramer – our not noticing echoing that same aspect of Gordon's 'crime'. Kramer is relegated to the background, a hospital extra ostensibly featured to provide authenticity to Gordon's role, and also to Zep's (who does offer the nudge 'he's an interesting person'). However, as the series progresses from SAW II to SAW III, Kramer moves closer and closer to centre stage, quickly becoming the franchise's iconic star. It is typical within horror properties that of all characters, it is the central antagonist that abides throughout the sequels: we all remember Jason, but can we name any of his victims? Likewise, it was Lecter's early years that were detailed in *Hannibal Rising* (2007), not Will Graham's or Clarice Starling's.

Kramer is a mad scientist archetype, who, in the seminal *Monsters and Mad Scientists*, Andrew Tudor characterises as 'the scientist who is obsessed with, and consumed by, his work, and who seeks and seems to have mastered the "secret of life itself"'.[34] Therefore, Jigsaw seeks to explore his victims' desire for life – 'how much blood will you shed to stay alive?' – and his traps and planning are certainly monomaniacal. Tobin Bell has the features of an academic; he is ordinary looking (not disfigured like Freddy, or Jason) and his pinched features suggest a careful intelligence. While Tudor took Frankenstein as his model, *SAW* develops the archetype; Jigsaw is a mad scientist of postmodern horror cinema.

POST MODERNITY

There is no place for the supernatural within the corporeal confines of torture porn. While the genre is narrow in its concerns, it is broad in its execution, representing specific fears exploding in bloody, *grand guignol* set pieces. Perhaps it can be argued that in order to accurately represent the fears of a modern, less innocent world, we need a new set of horror archetypes; the atavistic vampire and werewolf archetypes are irrelevant to the real-life horror of economic meltdown, terrorism and war that is played out daily across all forms of media. The genre characteristics of *SAW* provide scares that are more earthy than supernatural; pain, suffering, and gore abound, rather than the fantastical elements of earlier horror (even the new realism codes of 1970s horror featured zombies and quasi-supernatural bogeymen). The film jettisons the unexplained, the fantastique; its concerns are the horrors perpetuated by men upon men, explicitly 'real world' threats. Behind his flowing robes, John Kramer is alarmingly 'normal', and the *Hostel* films pointedly show their torturers to be family men – they are guys simply out for a good time, a corporate jolly. Minor entries within the cannon, such as *Captivity* (2007) and *Shuttle* (2008), use the 'switch reveal' that a supposed captive is actually the perpetrator of the victims' misery. In torture porn, the abiding face of horror is the banal, bland mug of the Everyman.

Nonetheless, *SAW* still contains many of the typical tropes and emblems that we would expect from the horror genre, with Jigsaw himself instigating much horror iconography first hand through the baroque design and gothic execution of his traps. It is easy to imagine that John Kramer could be a keen horror film fan; he writes his taunting instructions in bright red to mimic blood, his outfits include a scary pig get-up, and his puppet avatar is a macabre imp. He even (we assume) orders Zep to hide in Diana's closet; the cliché of the monster under the bed come to life. We could read this as a deliberate strategy on the part of Jigsaw; he uses the recognisable tropes of horror to terrorise his victims even further. Indeed, his victims are aware of the horror genre.

When confronted with the faux corpse of Jigsaw, Adam says 'It's the first dead body I've ever seen. They look different in real life, they don't move', showing his familiarity with horror film bodies that rise supernaturally (his words prefiguring his final, fatal shock). In the technology and media saturated world of *SAW*, where everyone is photographed or filmed, where anyone can be contacted at the end of a cell phone, and where even Jigsaw carves out a niche as a tabloid star,[35] a passing awareness of horror tropes and situations are inevitable. The film assumes our awareness of such time-honoured iconography as masks and blood, and creates new meanings in their usage. *SAW* itself exists within a rich horror legacy; James Wan references texts as esoteric as *Deep Red* (1975) (the Billy puppet) and *Black Christmas* (1974) (the eye peeping through the crack). (This writer can vouch for Wan and Whannel's enthusiastic interest in the horror genre after speaking to the pair about the sub-sub genre of scarecrow films at a convention.)

The critical cliché when referring to horror films and their gory situations is to characterise the texts as 'theatre of punishment'. However, the sobriquet is an apt descriptor for Jigsaw's puzzles as there is something of the showman to John Kramer. With apologies to *Peeping Tom* (1960), Jigsaw is the first multimedia serial killer. Jigsaw utilises gadgets, photographs, mobile phones; a plethora of audio/visual equipment to complete his plan. And when these accruements are not to hand, he is reliant on old-school smoke and mirrors: puppets, masks, shadows, even the old stand-by of deep voices. Again, these accruements are not used just to co-ordinate the misery, but to sadistically wring more terror out of the patrons of the traps. Its one thing to be bound in a reverse bear trap; another to be taunted by a creepy puppet as you struggle.

To take the analogy to its logical conclusion, we could even accept John Kramer as an auteur. He develops his own scripts, designs his stage settings, selects his stars and, finally, directs his own horror narratives first hand. He even has a stage name. Jigsaw is a cruel Roger Corman[36] who uses low budgets and ingenuity to create high body counts and spectacle, for real. Adam and Gordon's plight is even filmed and viewed from a safe distance within the diegesis. There is a clear suggestion that whoever is enacting the games is gaining a voyeuristic pleasure from the spectacle, he is watching just as we are. As Kerry says, 'Looks like our friend Jigsaw likes to book himself front row seats to his own sick little games'. Indeed, Amanda is even forced to watch a bespoke horror film, one in which the process of identification has drastic meaning for her; the separate dynamics of audience and text is distorted. To support this intent, mirrors are recurrent throughout the film, reflective surfaces that create duality. Indeed, when Adam shatters the mirror in the bathroom, it is revealed to be bogus, as it hides Zep's camera. Tapp compulsively watches and re-watches the Billy videos, becoming increasingly obsessed with the images on the small monitor screen. Ultimately though, it is the images of voyeurism, of watching suffering, that are the film's most pertinent mirror, as they parallel the audience's position; sitting back and enjoying the terror.

The stereotypical horror tropes embedded within the visceral excitement of its narrative, and the postmodern winks regarding audience voyeurism, are part of SAW's playful nature. The approach allows audiences to recognise typical codes and conventions, in order to negotiate familiar and unfamiliar narrative patterns. Steve Neale has asserted that we like genre products because they are 'the same, but different'. Further to this, Mark Kermode asserts that horror film fans enjoy decoding each new genre product 'in terms of a heritage of genre knowledge'.[37] Horror connoisseurs recognise familiar patterns; we like genre codes in SAW because they allow us to engage with the narrative on its own terms and on ours. It enables us to play its game.

FOOTNOTES

27. Welsh, 2002: 288–289
28. Biskind, 1998: 17
29. www.entertainment.timesonline.co.uk/tol/arts_and.../film/article6964114.ece
30. www.thesundaytimes.co.uk/sto/news/ireland/news/comment/article433687.ece
31. Burg. SAW VI DVD commentary, 2010
32. Wood in Jancovich, 2002: 29
33. www.uk.movies.ign.com/articles/103/1039913p1.html
34. Tudor, 1989: 29
35. Interestingly, the theme of media exploitation is neatly covered in the series finale, wherein a wily chancer promotes himself as a 'survivor' of Jigsaw, with celebrity appearances at support groups, and the glossy 'my story' autobiography of how he coped with his Jigsaw-inflicted escapade (S.U.R.V.I.V.E. My Story of Overcoming Jigsaw). Of course, he has not met Jigsaw at all … but he will. It is typical of SAW's reflective nature, and of the self-referential manner of the franchise, to finally present the monster himself as being exploited.

36. Roger Corman (1926–) a film director/ producer whose pioneering success with low budget exploitation films and subsequent mentoring of prodigious talent have earned him the position of American independent cinema's godfather. Although his early work was not exclusively aligned with horror, his later Poe cycle was critically acclaimed for its Gothic atmosphere.

37. Kermode in Barker and Petley, 1997: 57–66

AUDIENCES

The moral arguments concerning horror films are well documented. The most recognised (and most simplistic) of these arguments involves the 'effects debate', which is used to support concern of the potentially pernicious influence of horror upon its audience. Does continued exposure to images of violence and sustained threat influence and corrupt audiences? Is it possible that a horror film could be to blame for a social crime? In the mid-1980s in the UK, the Video Recordings Act (VRA) imposed more stringent modes of censorship on video releases (drawing a distinction between domestic and theatrical exhibition). The result of the VRA meant that at one point 75 videotapes were actually outlawed,[38] due to their perceived obscenity and potentially damaging effect. One Conservative Member of Parliament of the era claimed that exposure to horror could 'not only affect young people, but affect dogs as well'. The arguments surrounding the effects debate vary from the 'hypodermic syringe' proposition that a film could have a direct adverse influence on a viewer's outlook and actions after watching the text (inciting a viewer to ape the actions of a film murderer, for example), to the 'inoculation theory' that suggests that repeated viewings of horror texts can make audiences jaded and more accepting towards violent imagery.

Interestingly, the SAW films, or at least their marketing campaigns, would seem to subscribe to the passive 'inoculation' audience theory. The 'inoculation' hypothesis, or 'drip drip' theory, argues that continued exposure to violent images desensitises the audience, necessitating more extreme imagery in order to receive the requisite shock gratification. Each SAW movie certainly attempts to outdo its predecessor in terms of imaginative gore; the relatively scarce gore of SAW leading to the pig bath of SAW III, the autopsy of IV giving way to the flying intestines of SAW 3D. The series' marketing keys into this accumulative demand, in a sense postulating each film's USP as an increase in novel gore; SAW III's tagline is 'Suffering? You haven't seen anything yet'.

Conversely, what is interesting about the first SAW is the comparative lack of gore. If we overlook Amanda searching through intestines (actually a pig's uterus), the rest of the film's body horror is suggested rather than explicit. A personal favourite cringeworthy moment is when Kerry explains at the scene of Paul's death that he, 'cut himself so deep, we found traces of stomach acid on the floor', a scene not actually depicted, merely discussed. This awful detail plays insidiously on the mind; what we are forced to imagine is far more unpleasant than what we could ever be shown, because when we imagine, our own selves, rather than a screen avatar, are usually implicated. Higher production values in subsequent instalments would allow for more elaborate traps, but perhaps with each new innovation, the distance between spectacle and connection widens.

The original SAW exploits a multitude of fears. Clearly, there is the universal aversion to death; but also more specific terrors. Wan and Whannell wove their own particular personal dreads and phobias into the film. These include pediophobia (fear of dolls), taphophobia (fear of being buried alive), panthophobia (fear of suffering itself), swinophobia (fear of pigs), and, of course, nyctophobia – fear of the dark (during publicity for Insidious [2010], Whannell joked that the two made horror films because they were 'scared of everything'). The made-to-order nature of Jigsaw's traps allow for a broader use of fears; a variety of horror. There is something to get under everyone's skin in SAW's 99 minutes.

However, by the time of the third film, on the DVD's commentary, Leigh Whannell offered a mea culpa, 'the challenge is to make a film that implies fear, rather than disgusts the audience', and perhaps it is telling that the co-writer of the original SAW had by then taken a less hands-on approach with an executive producer credit. Personally, I would argue that the atrocities committed within SAW are horrific precisely because of their transferable nature: when we first see SAW, we instinctively wonder how we would fare in that dirty little bathroom. A severed limb, claustrophobia; these are features that an audience can all too easily imagine suffering. As the series progresses, the need for novelty has given way to larger, more elaborate traps that 'gross out' rather than 'scare'. The SAW series would eventually become a cinema of spectacle, culminating in 2010's SAW 3D. SAW's original gratification, however, was constructed through an intensely managed audience positioning; this is surely a major factor in its founding success. And, although SAW's relatively lo-fi intensity and character development did more to engage audiences' empathy, this positioning is continued throughout the series as a whole.

Alan Jones argues that 'the urge to scare oneself witless might seem masochistic. But exploring the notion of fear is revealing. We can open ourselves up to being scared if we know that no harm will befall us'.[39] Jones' use of the adjective 'masochistic' is especially pertinent to *SAW*. Perhaps a part of the repeated pleasures of *SAW*'s six sequels (to date) is witnessing the darker ingenuities of Jigsaw's new traps, subjecting ourselves to fresh fears to command or, at least, new pain to vicariously experience. Mark Burg, producer of the *SAW* franchise, recognises the empathetic pleasures of the contraptions, confirming that the traps are a proxy experience for viewers: 'When you talk to fans of the *SAW* movies, they always love the traps. One of the things that makes a great trap in the *SAW* franchise, is when the audience gets to be in the perspective of the person in the trap … the audience really thinks "what would I do if I were in this situation?"'[40]

The traps are filmed in such a way that the audience is positioned 'within' them, focusing on the player's panic, teasing us as to what we would do in the same situation. We do not see Amanda, Paul or Mark commit their sins; we only witness them play their games and with the exception of Amanda, die. This streamlines their presence, aiding their function as avatars for a vicarious experience.

If the scares in *SAW* are gruelling, then this is because *SAW* works upon a strict dynamic of identification, encouraging the audience to vicariously experience the terrors unfolding on the screen. The direct mode of address of *SAW*'s publicity, such taglines as 'We dare you again' and 'Suffering? You haven't seen anything yet…', is especially relevant.

Part of the series' narrative appeal is the multiple back stories of the *SAW* victims, which are alluded to by Jigsaw in his instructions. Each of Jigsaw's fatalities are captured due to what he perceives as the moral 'crimes' or 'transgressions' that they have committed ('sick of people who don't appreciate their blessings,' Jigsaw grumbles), and, indeed, the critic Joe Queenan has implied that if 'there was not somehow a sense in the *SAW*-style movies that the victims deserved to be dismembered' then the entire franchise 'would implode'.[41]

To generate an identification gratification, *SAW* plays upon our naturally transgressive natures. Perhaps, on some level, we feel that we ourselves deserve the punishment meted out on screen, or at least could qualify for it, which would consolidate our natural urge to see those who suffer escape their fate. Emphasising with the mechanical, monomaniacal killer is a bit like identifying with the funfair's rollercoaster as it big-dips us towards the ground. Instead, we peer fearfully into the abyss and witness our own screaming reflection within, siding with the human faces of Amanda, Dr Gordon, Adam, et al.

SAW the film is itself a 'trap'. Its narrative is unpredictable, and must be negotiated carefully. The *mise-en-scène* is confrontationally visceral and unpleasant. The process of identification that the film encourages has prompted us to soul search as to our own limits, our own transgressions. When the film has finished, we are relieved; and, perhaps, more self-aware – survivors ourselves.

As the series has progressed, the films have foregrounded their strategy of audience involvement, culminating in the shattered diegesis of SAW 3D's trailer, where the Pigmask character reaches into the cinema at the audience who are watching the film. Each SAW is event released at Halloween, and opening weekends often have a sense of occasion; gory, seasonal fun. The genre audience knows broadly what to expect within established patterns of narrative, but as to how the films will be delivered, how the traps will unfold, therein lies the novelty. It is entirely fitting that there is now a rollercoaster ride based on SAW, as the films themselves have primarily become thrill 'rides' for the audience.

In America, for its theatrical release, SAW suffered cuts in order to reduce its certification from a preclusive 'NC-17', to a more commercially friendly 'R' rating (the cuts were restored for DVD releases). In Britain, the BBFC classified SAW as 18, certifying it with no cuts made. The official BBFC comment states that, 'SAW was passed "18" for strong bloody violence' as it contravened the "15" certificate's established prohibition which states therein that, "Violence may be strong but should not *dwell on the infliction of pain or injury*. The strongest gory images are unlikely to be acceptable. *Strong sadistic violence* is also unlikely to be acceptable" (my italics).[42] This guideline could have been written with SAW in mind. The '18' certificate is a double-edged sword when we regard a genre film's reputation; on one hand, it is the badge of honour for any horror film, whose fans masochistically demand more realistic gore and violence tones, and sustained levels of terror (one of the teenage home invaders of *Cherry Tree Lane* [2010] asks his captives 'where are your 18s?' as he rifles through their DVD collection). However, it is also an exclusive certification, precluding the lion's share of the teen market. The '18' certificate necessitates a committed, niche audience to make its money, and to survive. SAW's international box office is rare for a film with such a streamlined target demographic.

NOTIONS OF LOOKING

> Whenever the movie screen holds a particularly effective image of terror, little boys
> and grown men make it a point of honour to look, while little girls and grown women
> cover their eyes or hide behind the shoulders of their dates.
> Linda Williams[43]

The title 'SAW' is a double entendre. It first refers to the actual tool that Gordon
utilises to remove his foot, but also connotes notions of looking, of watching. A teaser
poster interrogated audiences with the compound pun, 'Have you seen SAW?', the early
marketing establishing the text's themes of voyeurism. Within the film, various characters
observe and view each other: Tapp is watching Zep; Zep is watching Dr Gordon and
Adam; we are watching the intimate misery of the traps; and Jigsaw is watching us all.

From the dual meaning of its title onwards, SAW is fixated with notions of looking. The
theme of voyeurism is visually represented from the opening shots. We witness an eye,
in extreme close-up, shut: we can see the eye, but the eye is unable to see us. Screen-
filling close-ups on eyes are abundant within the film, most memorably during Amanda's
sequence, but also during Diana and Alison's ordeal; gagged, their wide eyes are the
only mode of expression. Mirrors also recur throughout the movie, surfaces within
surfaces. We see Gordon and Adam smash a mirror in the bathroom (which reveals
Zep's recording equipment), and they are evident in Gordon's household. Viewed from
the *noir* point of view that SAW invites (and considering the film's moral ideology), these
mirrors signify the duality of the film's characters: the person they are, and the person
that they could be. Jigsaw wants his captives to 'see' the error of their ways, which is only
possible through a hard-earned process of recognition.

The mirror motif has a secondary function, a symbolic reference to the film's tricksy
narrative conceits. The storyline loops back on itself, its non-linear narrative reproducing
earlier plot points in different light, reflecting what we know from different angles: Adam
does know Gordon; that guy in the hospital bed *was* interesting. This is a storytelling
technique that has been capitalised on by the sequels, where the events of the first film
have spun out into kaleidoscopic plot possibilities, seemingly stretched to box office
infinity.

Notions of looking are developed within *SAW* by the visual dynamic of the film; by its rudimentary, harsh style. Like Hitchcock's *Psycho* (1960), the original *SAW* short was filmed by television crews using television equipment. Previously a presenter for Australian youth television, Leigh Whannell took advantage of his contacts within the television industry:

> We'd worked at the ABC, which is like the Australian version of the BBC. We knew cameramen and people, just working in the industry for a couple of years meant we knew people. Like, we could ring up a camera guy and go, 'Could you come and help us do this for a couple of days?'[44]

The pared-down production values of television were evidently carried over to the film proper; the use of hand-held cameras, functional set designs and a close-up camera style of filming. Most of the film's visual aesthetic is drawn from the incendiary, gaudy glow of the lighting, a 'cheap' way to achieve a distinctive style that could only really work within the horror genre. The audience are ready to accept such hyper-real styling within these texts as they recognise the exaggerated, fantastic nature of the genre.

James Wan has spoken of his admiration for *The Exorcist* (1973) and its 'documentary style', and, in keeping with the new school of horror filming, *SAW* has distinct elements of this mode. Although popularised by the relatively recent *The Blair Witch Project* (1999), the documentary style in horror is not an especially new trope, having its roots in the Italian Cannibal Cycle of the 1970s, but it is an increasingly fashionable sub-genre; *The Last Exorcism* (2010), *Diary of the Dead* (2007), *Cloverfield* (2008) all being filmed explicitly in the 'found footage' style.

The reasons for the prevailing use of this style are threefold. Firstly, the method is cheap (which is especially attractive to genre film-makers). As digital cameras have become more lightweight and inexpensive, the possibilities for younger, first-time film-makers to create a show reel or even an entire first film, have opened up. Secondly, the style works well within horror as the approach supplies an immediacy, an 'in-your-face' propinquity that adds an abject layer of gratification (it is worth noting though, that this extra scare only happens when the film is of quality; many second-rate horrors have seized on the vogue for found footage, with mixed results, e.g. 2008's DTV *Cloverfield* cash-in, *Monster*, or even the underachieving *Diary of the Dead*). Thirdly, a modern world necessitates a modern style; in the twenty-first century a large proportion of our anxieties are already mediated through the filter of television, rolling news, amateur footage, or the darker margins of the internet. Horror has developed a new visual language, using a televisual mode of address, the grammar of 24/7 information. As Adam laments during *SAW*, 'the camera doesn't know how to lie'; it is the only 'truth' within the prevailing mendacity of *SAW*'s characters.

Although *SAW* is not explicitly of the 'found footage' genre, the film utilises many of its documentary codes. We can see these stylistic dimensions clearly in the sequences that portray Mark and Paul's death. These sequences are told in flashback, ostensibly from Dr Gordon's point of view (although, intriguingly, they show us information that he could not have known). The procedural element of the film is evident in the genre-specific lexis that is used by Gordon ('I was a suspect') and Kerry's terse summary, 'Victim's a 46-year old male'. There are then flashbacks *within* the flashbacks: we move from Gordon telling the story, to the detectives at the grisly aftermath, to the actual crime. These flashbacks are further evidence of the film's deft manipulation of time, and each period is filmed in a slightly different, distinctive style. Gordon is lit in cold blue, and the crime scene glows murky green. Furthermore, the camera positioning and mood of the scenes vary; the detectives are filmed in sober close-up, while the victims' camera uses a fuller depth of field, and a wider shutter speed.

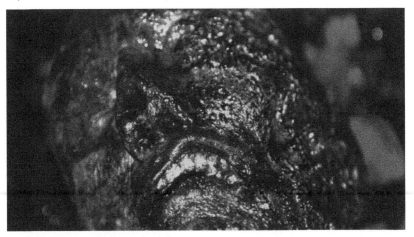

The miserable aftermath of Mark's death

The depth of field is expressive of the terrorised space that Mark and Paul die within; the chamber with its treacherous dimensions, the wire wool, the broken glass. However, the detectives are given close-ups to mimic the style of talking heads. They talk to each other, but we see mainly reaction shots; and their sentences are clipped, focused, as if we are following the crew of a television reality show. Interspersed with the sequences are crime photographs, black and white and fixated on forensic detail (a stylistic flourish that occurred by serendipitous accident; Wan used them in order to simply 'pad out' what he perceived as an otherwise possibly slack narrative). We see the traumatic results of Jigsaw's game through the medium of the pathologist's photography; an open wound, a charred skull. There is even the foley sound of a camera's whirr to create verisimilitude. Furthermore, there is the crime iconography of evidence bags and crime tape. These visual flourishes add a sense of veracity to these sequences. Within this pseudo-documentary style, Jigsaw is made to seem like a serious threat, as even the police seem taken aback by his exploits.

As the police make their way to Paul, they go down a narrow staircase. As they descend we watch them from an elevated dutch angle. This high-angle shot is located at the height and perspective of a closed-circuit camera; there is certainly something voyeuristic about the scene, as if we are seeing something that is not usually available to the public eye. Jigsaw himself has something of an all-seeing eye – he reminds Paul that, 'last month, [Paul] ran a straight razor across [his] wrists'. Presumably, this is the sort of action that Paul would have performed in private: the mind boggles as to how Jigsaw could be aware of such an event. However, as the film continues, we understand the breadth of Jigsaw's omniscience; he hires Adam and manipulates Zep (at least), and utilises surveillance tools. As the narrative draws to a close, and the two leads' secrets leak out, Adam tosses a bunch of images of Gordon: 'I can prove you never went anywhere near a hospital last night … I've been taking pictures of you for a few days now.' We see a montage of shots of Gordon sneaking about, even having a milkshake. Jigsaw is a supreme authority; no sin escapes his scrutiny.

In *SAW* there is the abiding suggestion that everyone is being viewed, and that their discretions will be punished. Technology has benefited authorities with hundreds of electronic cameras that survey our city streets. We are all familiar with the sensation of being watched by strange, unseen eyes. The axioms of Orwell's *1984* have become worn clichés; *SAW* incorporates our burgeoning uncertainties over authoritarian supervision within its themes of voyeurism and its pointed use of documentary *mise-en-scène*.

WAKING STATES AND NIGHTMARES

And all my days are trances,

And all my nightly dreams

Are where thy grey eye glances.

To One in Paradise Edgar Allen Poe[45]

The first act of terror that Jigsaw commits on his victims is to inject them with fast-acting soporifics. His primary modus operandi is to drug victims to sleep; who then wake up confined within their traps. We do not see the events that proceed their capture, we are only privy to the same information they are; we 'wake up' with them. (When we do find out how Adam and Gordon were initially captured, it is after the fact.) Sleep is a relevant motif within the film, as Jigsaw's intent is to shock his captives from the incognisant sleep of their lives, to wake them to the manifest possibilities of their existence. The film's imagery sustains this theme, as if the *mise-en-scène* itself is bending to Jigsaw's will.

As previously discussed, the first shot of SAW involves a closed eye in screen-filling extreme close-up and, following this established image, there follow several close-ups of eyes wide open in terror. The first words that Jigsaw speaks in the film are, 'Rise and shine, Adam,' and he continues the role of rouser when he informs Dr Gordon, 'This is your wake up call'. It is another measure of Jigsaw's sadistic control that he has dominance over his victims' physical, waking states. It is a measure of the victim's vulnerability also; we are never more defenceless than when asleep.

Sigmund Freud founded the accepted theory of dream when he suggested that they were indicative of the unconscious mind; that sleep revealed the latent mind's hidden desires and repressed fears. The waking world's conscious mind performs a protective function, repressing these emotions and feelings to the murky dungeon of the unconscious. However, when we slumber the dungeon door is opened, and we are prey to these hitherto suppressed emotions, now uninhibited.

As we sleep, our unconscious stalks the landscape of our inner cinema, and our past misdeeds and latent terrors tear at our dreams. The traps in SAW are living nightmares; for the victims to be woken up, the traps must be worked out and demons must be faced. The guilt narratives of the victims reach a nightmarish culmination in the traps; as Jigsaw says to Paul, 'Did you cut yourself because you truly wanted to die, or did you just want some attention? Tonight, you'll show me'. There is the sense that even the victims see the traps as fair game, or at least inevitable: no one ever argues as to how 'unfair' they are. In general, the victims of SAW just seem to get on with the gory business of working their way out, for better or worse, almost as if they have been partially expecting some sort of comeuppance. A vocal motif in torture porn films is the interrogative, 'Why are you doing this?', yet not one character in SAW's traps attempts to beg their way out.

Furthermore, in terms of how they are filmed, the torture rooms have the ethereal, nightmare lighting of Italian horror, and are in sumptuous contrast to the dull 'waking' world. Shadow and light fuse to a nocturnal, soporific glow, 'techno torture lairs' in the words of Roger Ebert.[46] The 'sleep' theme is further fortified by the repeated iconography of beds in the film. There is John's hospital bed, Diana's kiddie bedroom, the motel where Gordon meets Carla, and also the bed that Alison and Diana are held captive against. These visual signifiers are subliminal reminders of sleep and its potential treacheries, which wait in the bedroom closet like the perfidious Zep. The audience is positioned to process the traps, then, as a form of dream logic, allowing us to accept the film on its own, fantastic genre terms.

The recurring character pose of the torture porn genre is of victims being seated as atrocities are imposed upon them. There is Amanda in SAW, Josh in Hostel. There are also repeated incidents of characters stuck where they are and cringing as they watch others being tortured; this happens in Wolf Creek (2005), and throughout the SAW sequels. The attempts to parallel the viewing position of the audience are clear.

Whenever we visit the cinema, we are privy to reverie; the act of watching a film itself, any film, is to participate in a sort of collective dream. We sit in comfort, in a dark room, on a soft, plush seat, and take part in a suspension of belief, a mass trance. However, in SAW, this dynamic is exploited more specifically, as our predicament mirrors that of the protagonists. Like the torture rooms, the cinema is a dark chamber, filled with screams and suffering from the screen in front. We cannot leave the film – if we do, our experience will be incomplete; it is imperative to stay and conclude the experience. Like the characters, we are also invited to piece together the puzzle, to endure as the victims do, to play the game.

Furthermore, the sense of claustrophobia that SAW used so effectively has been increasingly developed in the diminishing horizons of modern horror. 2010 alone saw the release of Buried, set entirely in a coffin, and Devil, which barely retreats from its elevator milieu; while [REC] 2 is set within a series of cramped, enclosed interiors. The Paranormal Activity films contrast their spiritual forbear The Blair Witch Project of a decade earlier by focusing their terrors to single domestic locations, rather than wide-open, overpowering space. Perhaps the 'claustrocore'[47] movement has gained credence due to the insular, reduced nature of our lives; or at least, our interaction with others. Teenagers socially interact, watch films, consume music, all from the digital screens of their laptops, and the various multimedia platforms that it uses to exploit and command their attention. This 'shrinking' is maintained by their MP3 players, and the mobile phones that are extensions of their own limbs, completing an insular outlook, and further reducing social horizons. 'Claustrocore' is modern horror; with its HD close-ups and chiaroscuro lighting, it is reliant on the new technologies of smaller cameras to film its tight crevices. Its limited spheres are reflective of our circumscribed, cyber world.

FOOTNOTES

38. Kerekes and Slater, 2000: 67
39. Jones, 2005: ppix
40. Burg, SAW V DVD commentary, 2009
41. www.guardian.co.uk/film/2010/oct/22/queenan-horror-cliches-ring
42. www.bbfc.co.uk/BVF201470/
43. Williams in Doane et al, 1984: 83

44. www.uk.movies.ign.com/articles/561/561009p2.html

45. Poe, 1997: 31

46. www.rogerebert.suntimes.com/apps/pbcs.dll/article?AID=/20041028/
    REVIEWS/40923005/1023

47. www.theincrediblesuit.blogspot.com/2010/09/boo-hoo-im-trapped-is-new-boo-hoo-im.html

SAW AND SEQUELS

In his *BFI Companion to Horror*, the estimable Kim Newman remarks that horror is comedy's 'closet kin'; and, indeed, many horror films incorporate elements of humor to leaven their intensity.[48] *The Evil Dead* (1981), a notorious 'nasty', contains elements of sparse slapstick; slasher films often contain a 'goof' kid within their cliques. However, *SAW* is entirely humorless; there are no wisecracks or pratfalls to provide momentary relief; there is no relief from the grim severity of Jigsaw's moral quest. The unremitting nature of *SAW*, and, indeed, the entire torture porn *oeuvre* is what limits the subgenre. Torture porn is monomaniacal, dedicated to an effective, but incredibly simplistic, mode of horror. As a viable cinematic commodity, the genre seems to be at the end of its cycle; the vogue now seems to be for the short, sharp shocks to be found within the domestic settings of *Paranormal Activity* and *The Last Exorcism*, with audiences relating to scares that disrupt the most mundane and blameless of 'everyday' milieu. Wan and Whannell's *Insidious* is a superlative example of this sub-genre.

However, *SAW* has endured for over half a decade; with six sequels to date. In fact, its second sequel made more money than the original film (*SAW III* accumulated a worldwide gross of $163,876,815 compared to *SAW*'s $103,096,345), perhaps proving that the original film's notoriety led to word-of-mouth anticipation. At the time of writing, the combined global takings for the films (not including DVD releases) are $758,557,095. There is a complexity at work within the films' marketing, and the consequent sustaining of *SAW*'s lure. Zygi Kamasa, head of Lionsgate, suggests that the return of audiences to the *SAW* franchise is reliant on an ever-developing storyline, which evolves with each new chapter. '*SAW* is rare', he says:

> Historically, franchises deteriorate over time in terms of business, mainly because the makers get lazy and just churn out another same old *Halloween*. We raise the bar in each film and we also *hold something back* so we've got something *juicy for the next instalment the year after*.[49] (my italics)

This quote is not only suggestive of a calculated, focused business plan, but also of a respect for the audience; the awareness that audiences value story and development. A study of *SAW* would be incomplete without an overview of its heritage; its unfolding narrative, and its on-going box-office business.

The *SAW* spin-offs have the distinction of being both sequels *and* prequels to the original film. There is the implication, reinforced by marketing, that the original experience will be consolidated with each new instalment. Indeed, following the franchise, each instalment offers new narrative information that supplements our understanding of the original plot. *SAW II* shows us John Kramer pulling himself from the wreckage of a car crash, undergoing the sort of endurance test he will force his victims to relive. In *SAW III* we are shown, in flashback, John Kramer walking in a park with an attractive woman; this enigma is not satisfied until *SAW IV*, wherein we discover that it is the loss of their unborn child that is the initial trigger to the Jigsaw persona. In *SAW V* we learn that it is Amanda Young herself who was indirectly responsible for the death of this child; thus being accountable for the creation of Jigsaw. *SAW V* also shows Hoffman being retconned[50] into the franchise; it was he who helped Jigsaw capture Paul. *SAW 3D* brings the final off-the-wall revelation that it is Gordon who has also been a franchise long accomplice to Kramer.

With each instalment's promise of 'revealing the full story', the franchise is at least distinctive in the way it recycles already familiar narrative pleasures, delivering them in 'novel' ways. And, as well as providing a unique, ever-unfolding plotline, which is in itself attractive and rewarding for fans, the retroactive narrative allows the film-makers the luxury of covering over their own plot holes (it always was slightly ridiculous that a dying man would be able to overcome and transport a man of Paul's size).

In the horror sequel *Scream 2* (1997), a character protests that 'sequels ruined the horror genre'. One can certainly see his point when we look at the ever-diminishing returns of the infamous *Friday the 13th* sequels, or DTV fodder like the recent *Lost Boys* (2008) or *30 Days of Night (Dark Days)* (2010) spin-offs. However, the character's outburst was from the aesthetic point of view of the fan purist, not a financial one: from a business angle, the rant is entirely contestable. It is arguable that, far from being ruinous, sequels are in fact the financial lifeblood of the horror genre.

The horror genre was established through sequelisation. Between 1931 and 1948, Universal studios made eight films featuring Victor Frankenstein's lumbering creation, four featuring Dracula and six featuring The Wolf Man. These cycles were a mixture of on-going narratives and semi-remakes: the Frankenstein films follow a coherent storyline, while the Dracula sequence is less consistent (*Son of Dracula* [1943] stands alone, an early 'reboot'), and, indeed, the characters would cross over and do battle with each other (*House of Frankenstein* [1944], *Frankenstein Meets the Wolf Man* [1943]). These were the films that established horror as a viable commercial industry, created the templates for the modern genre and provided its lasting archetypes: the mad scientist, the man/animal hybrid and the creature who feeds from humans.

Returning to *Scream 2*, the film was itself culpable of initiating the late 1990s cycle of postmodern 'slasher' movies. During the film's reflective narrative, its outspoken character Randy outlines the 'rules' that horror sequels should follow: 'Number one, the body counts are always bigger. Number two, the death scenes are always more elaborate, more blood, more gore; your core audience just expects it.' The *Scream* argument suggests that a horror sequel's appeal lies within the second text being an augmented version of the first, the apparent pleasures of the initial text repeated in a manner that further emphasises their attributes.

When an audience returns to see a sequel to a film that they have enjoyed, there are several reasons why they may do so. Firstly, they may want to duplicate the viewing pleasure of the original text (*Paranormal Activity 2* [2010]). This is perhaps the most prominent reason. Secondly, the previous film may have ended on a narrative cliffhanger, and the film that follows satisfies those narrative enigmas as part of an over-arching narrative; this is a rarer proposition, as the film-makers need to be confident enough in their original product to guarantee a separate continuation of it (so we are more likely to see this occur within big-budget family affairs such *Harry Potter* or *Star Wars*). Finally, the audience may identify strongly with a particular character in the original text (for example, Indiana Jones), and wish to see this character again in further productions.

Sequels are attractive for studios because they have a pre-sold quality; producers know how successful the first movie was, and already have an idea how to market the sequel product to its core audience. When money is invested in a film before it is released (on production costs such as script, crew and location) this is known as 'sunk costs' – costs that, in the event of the movie's failure, cannot be recouped. Developing movies is an expensive business, which perhaps accounts for the increasing paucity of chance-taking in Hollywood. Sequels reduce the risk factor, as studios can feel confident that they have already built a decent-sized audience from the original film and that the 'brand' of the movie has already captured the public imagination.

This goes doubly for remakes, and the glut of recent Seventies horror 're-imaginings' in particular. Initially, which horror fan could resist seeing a Seventies horror classic remade with Noughties technology and studio budgets? Older horror audiences are lured by the promise of such a cinematic 'make-over'; the fresh experience of watching the original film again could be captured: the same concept, but with new scares and bloodier shocks. Younger horror audiences were drawn by the excitement of finally seeing these versions of fabled texts on a big screen; the more casual, uninitiated observer simply viewed a new horror film. While hardcore horror fans may bemoan the 'artlessness' of such endeavors, it is worth remembering that even Hitchcock was not above remaking own films, with 1934 and 1956's *The Man Who Knew Too Much*. In any case this remake cycle is not a 'new' strategy: Hammer remade and repositioned the 1930s Universal films for 1960s audiences. Horror texts stand up well to remakes, as an individual text's particular themes, and the fear it inspires, can be transposed to new and different social contexts. Most crudely, the *The Hills Have Eyes* films (1977 / 2006) reflect the social ramifications of Vietnam and the 'War on Terror'. It is likely that in a decade or so, *SAW* itself will have its own reboot.

Furthermore, it is arguable that audiences are conditioned to expect sequels from their horror originals; certainly, the marketing machine behind the *SAW* franchise are aware of the on-going spin-off potential of their product, sowing clues in one film that are exploited a year later during the following instalment.

Of all genres, perhaps horror lends itself to sequelisation more readily than other types of narrative. The opened-ended nature of the storylines invites narrative dissatisfaction, and the simple, earthy dynamics of the plot are easily replicated, allowing for repeated pleasures. Romero's *Dead* series all feature the zombie-versus-human opposition with blunt political relevance, but each sequel relocates these foundations of the franchise within novel dressings; be it a mall, an island or a road movie. Horror audiences are typically young, and it is this audience who most seek reassurance and gratification through repeated cultural experiences (playing the same artist's music, association with a particular fashion brand). Alan Jones even locates the experience of being an adult horror fan as one of nostalgia, or arrested development nourished by sordid repeated pleasures:

> I've been a horror fan since I was 10 years old. Fans want to recreate the feeling they had when they saw an '18' rated film for the first time. I like the gore, I like the jumping out of my seat, I want to see something that I can't look at but can't tear my eyes away from. I want that moment to happen to me again and again.[51]

Since some audience's main pleasure of horror films is the visceral experience of being scared (the marketing of *Paranormal Activity* realises this, and its trailers prominently feature hysterical audiences reacting to preview screenings of the film), the nuts and bolts of plot is perhaps of less importance than the gut sensation. Romantic comedy, for instance, necessitates a neat, incontestable narrative resolution; the union of its 'star-crossed lovers'. As the plot is driven by the two protagonists' contrived distance, a sequel would necessitate a divorce, which would lead to another reconciliation, which would stretch audience credulity: the pleasure of these films is believing in the escapist possibility of *true* love. Rom-com sequels are rare, and indeed, the most successful romance franchise of recent times – the *Twilight* saga – borrows its iconography from horror.

Like its undead denizens, the horror film repeatedly returns from the grave, coming back to haunt our minds and multiplexes. Another reason for this mutability is surely due to the intrinsically metaphorical nature of the horror film's threat. For instance, the vampire is equally at ease being a representation of xenophobic fears (*Nosferatu*) as a symbol of abstained sexuality (*Twilight*). The traps of *SAW* are easily transferable to new and more current malaises and fresh sins. Talking about the 'moral issues' of the victims, producer Jason Constantine proudly talks of the characters in the opening scene of *SAW VI* having, 'contributed in some way to our financial recession'. The two characters are both loan bankers, and their game involves them having to shed a literal pound of flesh.

However, the sequel business is not a guarantee of success, with some sinking without a trace (*Hostel 2* was a notorious flop, and put paid to any hopes of a theatrical franchise, with 2012's *Hostel 3* being released on DVD). If a studio has enough confidence in the product's potential to bankroll a sequel, then the goal is a franchise; if this is to be at all possible then the sequel must deliver, not only in terms of audience turn out, but in terms of audience satisfaction. The two factors are not necessarily connected: unlike a meal, you pay for a film *before* you consume it; one cannot 'send it back'. A film can conceivably enjoy a huge opening weekend, but audiences may be dissatisfied with what they have already paid for (or, if the meal was bad, the eatery will not enjoy your repeat business). While the studio may be able to release one bad sequel, it will perhaps not get away with another. A franchise is a lucrative investment for a studio; the sequel that ruins it kills the goose that could lay further golden eggs. (There is, however, a cinematic legacy other than theatrical release, one that has become increasingly vital in the age of downloaded movies. At the time of writing, the digital streaming site, Netflix, accounts for 22% of American internet traffic.)[52]

The age of the blockbuster franchise was the 1980s, when the twin technologies of cinema and video dominated. Currently, however, it is more likely for a franchise to exist within a direct-to-video (DTV) context. The DTV market works on a lower budget principle; no theatrical release means reduced marketing, and a diminished need for glossy production values. As stated earlier, this was the assumed destiny for the first *SAW* film. There is a substantial sequel market for DTV releases, which are exclusively designed to exploit the original text's remaining niche audience. PJ Pesce, the director of four DVD sequels, explains the opportunistic nature of this 'brand' market:

> Sometimes an independent producer will make a movie, and studio marketing guys will see it and go, 'Huh, I'll tell you what, if we name this thing *8mm 2*, we can immediately sell 200,000 copies based on that title alone'.[53]

The sequel to *Lost Boys* (1987) was released DTV in 2008, and made back it's meagre $5m budget within a month of release, clearly capitalising on a niche nostalgia market. Lionsgate is particularly involved with this method of distribution, releasing *American Psycho 2* in 2002, and distributing *Cabin Fever 2* (2009) and *Open Water 2* (2006) DTV.

There are few recourses that a franchise can take to introduce novelty, and it is often a mark of a franchise's desperation when its sequel reaches for gimmicks: *Jason X* - 'Jason in Space'!; *Jaws 3D* (and, er, *SAW 3D* – can we assume that this film is simply a bow to the current vogue for the technique?). A special mention should therefore go to *Halloween 3: Season of the Witch*. This 1982 second sequel to what was at the time one of independent horror's most successful films bore no relation to the earlier films, jettisoning the iconic bogeyman and the cat-and-mouse narrative. It was instead a supernatural horror about inter-dimensional terrorism. Audiences were bemused, and by 1988's *Halloween 4*, Michael Myers was back. What is difficult for a modern studio, then, is to provide just the right blend of the familiar and the novel. Looking at the *Nightmare on Elm Street* cycle, franchise 'star' Freddy Krueger was just not scary by 1987's part 3. How could he be? Initially, he had been a shadowy presence, unseen clearly until the final reel of the 1984 original. However, by becoming one of horror's most recognised icons, his capacity to frighten was diluted and the character was made progressively sillier, eventually becoming a camp icon. There was still the familiar premise of fatal dreams, but with the novel angle of a pop culture star doing the killing, and this 'new' incarnation of Freddy Krueger lasted for five more spin-offs. Over in *Friday the 13th* land, the unsettling brutality of the original film was replaced by more and more outlandish killings; the presumable pleasure being how victims die, not the shock of it happening (at that point though, the formula must have been common to even the most casual horror fan). Analogously, as the *SAW* series progresses, the traps are filmed in more detail; the camera lingers on gory outcomes, the suffering of the victim. The inevitable pit and the pendulum nod in *SAW V* trades not only on the swinging suspense of the scythe falling, but the detail of fingers being crushed, which is the unpleasant price for stopping the trap. Conversely, the traps in *SAW* work consistently on a win/lose equation: if she does not open the bear trap/Amanda's head will be crushed; if Mark does not find the combination/he will die by poison. The first film's traps are generally a 'race against time', a dynamic underlined by the continuous motifs of watches and clocks. The later films' traps are more sadistic, involving more bloodletting and physical pain; the victims are dying from the moment the trap is initiated.

For *SAW* then, the continued appeal is arguably the miserable ingenuity of Jigsaw's traps, and how people die or survive them; along with Jigsaw himself, who has wisely been used sparsely throughout the series (protecting his brand value mystique). *SAW* is interesting in terms of its sequalisation. Unlike the standard plot trajectory of horror film sequels (the rinse/repeat cycle of Jason dies, is resurrected, causes havoc, is defeated … for now), the *SAW* franchise writes an overarching, on-going plot, peeling back layer upon layer of narrative with each new instalment. What may seem offhand and irrelevant in part II becomes a crucial plot point in part IV and indeed, we discover at the end of *SAW III* that the events of that film have been running parallel to the suffering of old Adam and Dr Gordon from the original film. This is an element of anticipation that Lionsgate is fully aware of, and had thus incorporated it into its marketing; *SAW V's* tagline promises that 'In the end, the pieces will fit together'.

IN THE END ALL THE PIECES WILL FIT TOGETHER

SAW V's DVD cover

It's always interesting to know when audiences start piecing together who's doing what in the film. Mark Burg[54]

Each of the *SAW* films pick up immediately where the previous film's narrative ended, and each new episode brings fresh narrative information pertaining to what we have seen in the previous films. This intricate narrative sequencing is one of the franchise's major fan-pleasing aspects; each film returns to the warehouse of the first film, and the audience is given further revelation as to Jigsaw's motivations, and a new understanding of the 'behind the scenes' action.

As each film in the franchise must be congruous with the various flashbacks and repeated scenes it will house, the original style *SAW* has to be meticulously recreated for each instalment. In fact, for a later sequel, long after the original bathroom set where Adam and Gordon had suffered had been destroyed, the setting was required again, so the production team had to *borrow* the mock set that the film-makers of the *Scary Movie* parodies had created, driving it from California to Toronto! Fans would not forgive a less stringent attention to detail – the core success of all franchises always relies on the patronage of the hardcore, niche audience. The *SAW* franchise lapsing in terms of its complex narrative and recurrent *mise-en-scène* would be akin to the *Transformers* franchise toning down the spectacular destruction: a betrayal of brand values.

This intricate narrative offers multiple gratifications for the audience; the pleasure of recognition, and involvement ('Ah, I see now!'), and, conversely, the uncertainty and disorientation inherent to horror ('So, it didn't *quite* happen as I saw it'). The films are always one step ahead in terms of their complex narrative; the audience are never comfortably certain where they stand with the plotlines of *SAW*. This alpha narrative hook is another reason for the consistent return of audiences; 'What happens next?' *SAW VI* ends with the cliffhanger that Hoffman is *not* killed by Jill Tuck; he has managed to work his way out of the reverse bear trap, and his revenge is set up for part VII. At this point in the franchise, the producers had enough bankability to be able to plan certain narrative points ahead.

Indeed, Hoffman was merely a bit player in *SAW III*, but has worked his way up to the franchise's central villain by *SAW 3D*. The trap conceit has remained and, as Randy from *Scream* may well argue, the traps have become accordingly more elaborate, resulting in more blood and gore in their execution. However, what has gone on around the traps is what has provided novelty and interest; a narrative universe of interacting characters and interlocking, multi-causal plots. We have focused on different major characters in each instalment, each completing their varied character arcs. We see Jigsaw's wife as a beguiling enigma in *SAW III*'s flashback; in *SAW V*, she is a mystified bystander; in *SAW VI*, an avenging angel; and, of course, in *SAW 3D*, she dies as a victim. The satirical website cracked.com offered a day in the life of Jigsaw, mocking the series' overtly complex narrative (see overleaf).

Cracked.com plans out Jigsaw's day

Moreover, each sequel carefully builds on themes established in the first film: themes of retribution, survival, order and control are explored in each instalment, but also the more personal themes that gave the original film its emotional identity. The theme of fatherhood, in particular, is expanded on; from Adam and Gordon's absent dads, the narrative elaborates to pinning the moment when John Kramer lost his child to his eventual descent towards becoming Jigsaw. Eric Matthews is punished in *SAW II* for his poor parenting; and *SAW IV*'s main trap is an elaborate revenge on the insurance company head who denied an ill father a chance to live.

Giving the 'health insurance' plot point from *SAW VI* further attention, we see that this is another example of the films' continual mistrust of capitalised industry. Throughout the series, we witness several faceless corporations' exploitation of the 'little man' (the housing insurance cover up of *SAW V* is another example). When looking at the series' continued success, it is important to take into account not only the slavish recreation of style, and the twisting of previous narrative plot points, but also the conscious deepening of the original's themes. This shows a clear awareness of fan 'ownership' of the movies, the producers valuing the fan's desire for continuity.

MARKETING

Rom-coms build their genre properties around stars, such as Jennifer Aniston or Sandra Bullock. The horror film builds its brand identity around its antagonists. When Paramount developed the *Friday the 13th* franchise, they talked about the Jason mask as being the 'Nike swoosh of horror'. Jigsaw himself comes ready branded; there is the irresistibly iconic Billy puppet, the urgent slashed font of the *SAW* logo, and the pig masks. It is possible to buy *SAW* mugs, Billy dolls and various T-shirts. It is curious that horror films lend themselves to branding and merchandising opportunities so readily. At any comic shop, patrons are able to buy a model or toy of any of the major serial killers of horror cinema, and T-shirts bearing reproductions of horror posters are commonplace uniform in rock subcultures. Horror encourages an intense identification and passionate following, as the genre is deeply personal. There is a clear active response to horror, an interactive dynamic between fans and text. Purchasing and displaying this merchandise is a way of announcing this fandom, as is publicising your genre know-how to other fans. (At the 2010 FrightFest film festival in London, critic Alan Jones, the organiser, complimented me on the *Dark Night of the Scarecrow* T-shirt I was wearing, almost causing me to go into fanboy cardiac arrest.) The iconic aspirations of modern horror marketing are attempts to forge for each particular film a unique identity in a highly competitive environment: a recognisable brand, a memorable design for the killer's mask, create impact upon the increasingly viral channels of film marketing.

Of course, the chief marketing tool for any major or independent release today is the official website. The *SAW* website *officialsaw.com*, which, at the time of writing advertises the seventh incarnation of the film, fulfils the dual criteria of a modern website; to serve as a nexus for fans, and a multimedia space to advertise the primary text. Fans can primarily visit the site as a first stop for *SAW* information and goodies; titbits concerning casting and forthcoming plots, exclusive footage, trailers. While they are there, the captive audience (so to speak) can buy exclusive merchandise in a link that takes users to the official *SAW* eBay auction. This merchandise is rather esoteric, and clearly intended to exploit the obsessive nature of the *SAW* fan base; recent items for sale include a Cary Elwes autograph, or used tickets for the *SAW 3D* premiere.

The *SAW* website provides forums for these enthusiasts to discuss the intricacies of the films, to argue the finer points of the traps, and to create meaning from the many clues embedded within the *SAW* mythology. The domain's forum space provides fans with a sense of community, but it also serves to consolidate the hardcore audience of the film, creating loyalty for *SAW*. The communal nature of horror is further suggested by the site's 'agency' page, wherein addresses are provided from where festival/convention organisers can book stars of *SAW*, or props from the film ('we can make your event stand out'). Other synergous goodies include an advert for the American Red Cross –

Tobin Bell forcefully intoning 'This year we want more of your blood,' before helpfully reminding audiences, 'if it's Halloween, it must be *SAW*'. There is also an extensive picture gallery here to encourage and maintain fandom.

The creative design of *officialsaw.com* is detailed and clearly has high production values. It continues the meticulous branding of the franchise with due care and attention to detail; the main image is of a rollover buzzsaw that moves from left to right as the cursor passes over it, and rolling over icons emits a gleaning metallic chink. The movie's score swells in the background. There are sections for each film, with synopses and trailers for each text. The site is rather an immersive experience, a thorough advertisement for each of the films. *SAW* even has an 'official' fan site – *officialsawnews.com*, 'the fan site authorised by Twisted Pictures'. The webmaster has been allowed unprecedented access to shoots, sets, after-show parties: an aspirational position for anyone with more than a passing interest in cinema (this site does, of course, also feature links to official merchandise).

Other, less polished, fan sites, such as *sawgame.net* and *www.angelfire.com/scary2/saw2* mainly provide communal opportunities for fans to discuss plot enigmas and 'favourites'. Polls range from the plausible:

Which unanswered question do you think should have been answered?

The fans pick: Who were the other two Pigheads that attacked Hoffman?

to the twee:

Where do you think John Kramer deserves to go to?

The fans pick: Heaven

The internet presence of *SAW* is as slick and creative as the films. The obsessive nature of the horror fan allows the sites to build on this fixation, mobilising to aggressively promote the films' universe, and sell the most esoteric of related 'merch'.

A film's marketing campaign, however, usually begins with a poster. It is the poster that is exhibited in cinema foyers, the poster that displays the website domain, and the poster that establishes the themes and plot of the primary text. For many film fans, the anticipatory event of scrutinising the film poster is part of the overall experience of consuming the film. A look at the poster campaign for the original film is evidence of the deliberate branding of the SAW franchise, and the keen styling of the primary text.

It is the duty of any marketing department to present the unique themes and style of a film to target audiences in such a distinct way that they will immediately recognise the brand, and hopefully become attracted to it. The competition for audiences is fierce for any cinematic text, but especially for horror, which has an already prohibited potential audience due to age restriction; and for an independent horror film, there are further complications. The main obstacle for independent films is distribution and promotion. Traditionally, this has been to the advantage of major studios, which have more capital at their disposal. Horror posters cannot usually rely on star quality to attract viewers, and since its genre codes are often bluntly archetypal, it must often create a sense of innovation or a promise of something different to impress a possible audience. Establishing a film properly to the right audience is crucial. Often, this novelty takes the form of implied shock or gore, but in the case of SAW there is a genuinely distinct style at work.

Unlike pricey billboards and public advertising, poster exhibition is free within cinemas. Taking advantage of this avenue, and, in keeping with the movie's multiple narrative threads, the poster campaign for SAW made use of a triptych:

SAW's promotional triptych 2004

In terms of its colour scheme, the poster uses the enduring horror monochrome of red and black: danger and darkness, blood and death. Its weird characters are pale and washed out. In horror, conveying the genre of the text, rather than its representation codes, is paramount to marketing concerns; although exceptions are usually made for scantily-clad young women (true to type, the reduced one-sheet used the primary image of Shawnee Smith to lure audiences).

The complex narrative unique selling point of the film is, however, conveyed here, albeit in a subtle manner. The tripling of the one-sheets meant that the three posters would perhaps have to be displayed in a fragmented manner within cinema foyers; casual observers would have to 'seek out' the next letter to see what the title of the film was;

mirroring the viewing experience of 'looking' for clues. It is unusual, but not unheard of, for cinemas to receive multiple posters for the same film; most usually arrive in quad- and one-sheet formats. However, Lionsgate's marketing team were savvy in producing a series that would only spell the title of the advertised film when displayed together; the tripled poster thus gives the impression of an 'event' release.

The font looks as if it was scrawled in haste; this conveys the urgency of horror (and chimes with Amanda's intense glare), but also hints towards the artisan nature of Jigsaw's traps. The stylish imagery is startling and actually quite unsettling; it certainly has an idiosyncratic visual impact.

We see an attractive woman in danger, which since the English Gothic tradition has been the abiding female representation of horror, and so the image conforms to audience expectations. We could even perhaps assume that this is a Proppian princess; she certainly looks like she needs saving. The trap is shadowed, creating enigma codes. At the time the film was released, torture porn was in its nascence, and such devices were a novelty to the poster's target audience; the pleasure of genre involves an established gratification being delivered in a distinctive way. Amanda looks at something before her in terror, not at us; this connotes a sense of voyeurism that is key to the genre. We are observing her in these terrible moments. Unpleasantly, there is a focus on the character's flesh; a vague sense of sex appeal is communicated for the stereotypically male demographic.

What is also typically expressive of genre is the representation of Billy and Pigmask. Pigmask is perhaps potentially the most familiar representation. With the vile facade obscuring the character's face, Pigmask is a stock horror film character; the masked killer. There is something queasily knowing about the mask's 'smile' too, smugly assuming an understanding of the audience. Billy, being a puppet, is a little more unusual. Although dolls have had distinct roles in *Magic* (1978) and *Dead of Night* (1945), it is still rare for a movie to draw upon pediophobia (although James Wan would expand upon fear of dolls in his next horror project, *Dead Silence*). Billy is centralised within the triptych, and positioned above the 'A' of *SAW*; the point of which sharpens into a pyramid peak over which Billy presides. This communicates Billy (who is Jigsaw's avatar) as the twisted master of whatever ceremonies *SAW* has in store, an image supported by the dapper dress code – a tux and bow-tie – denoting status. His is the only image that has direct address; its red eyes staring right out at us, as if to seek out the audience's moral transgressions. The film's tagline is strategically placed on the Billy poster – 'How much blood would you shed to stay alive?' – to reinforce Billy's piercing visual address. The ruthless binary opposition of Jigsaw's interrogative (related in the film as 'Live or die, the choice is yours') is essentially the narrative urge of horror boiled down to its merciless essentials: survive or die. SAW puts the survival instinct centre stage; in this sense it is a minimalist horror, one that all audiences can relate to on an immediate, visceral level.

For the film's sequels, the central poster images are that of Tobin Bell as Jigsaw, the film sequence's common denominator. However, there has been a consistently playful, creative aspect to the subsequent posters. Unlike the grim original campaign, a dark sense of humour is evident in consequent promotion; the torn-off double fingers denoting the first sequel, tripled teeth for III, the Jigsaw skin-mask of V. Having established character, narrative and tone with SAW, the succeeding posters can afford to play with pre-sold qualities; the original campaign establishes the film as something strange, complex and deeply unpleasant – hardcore horror.

The trailer for SAW, however, is less oblique. Building upon the enigma codes of the poster campaign, the trailer consequently gives a clearer sense of the film's narrative, and introduces the film's major characters.

Whereas the poster campaign for the film is drawn from an original, purpose-taken series of photographs, and given a bespoke design, the SAW trailer is a prolonged but hastily edited sequence of pre-existing clips from the film. The trailer (which is two minutes long) begins with the scene in which Adam is kidnapped by Pigmask. This opening is rather effective, as the flashes to light from blackness utilise the darkness of the auditorium. Immediately, we are given a digestible Todorovian premise – man is kidnapped. We are also privy to the film's themes of captivation and voyeurism within this short sequence (Adam uses a camera to light his flat). What follows is a montage that shows all of the major characters, but, most significantly, Adam and Gordon in their cell, first from the film's dominant point of view, but also from Zep's. Interspersed with the montage are a series of intertitles that pertain to Jigsaw: 'Madman… Voyeur… Psychopath… Prophet…', which conclude with the direct address, 'It's his game….

And your move.' These intertitles arrange the disruptions around a single, unknown antagonist, the requisite boogeyman.

By streamlining the narrative, the trailer skillfully creates a sense of enigma. We ask who is doing this, and wonder as to what his impetus is. It seems more involved than the Oedipal issues of most horror slashers; there are complex motivations suggested, which in itself is a USP. If the film *SAW* is ultimately a mystery, then the trailer is its first clue.

The game begins.

FOOTNOTES

48. Newman, 1996: 11
49. www.guardian.co.uk/film/2009/oct/15/saw-horror-movie-franchise
50. 'To retcon' is to retell a part of an established narrative with new information.
51. www.entertainment.timesonline.co.uk/tol/arts_and.../film/article7009504.ece
52. www.wired.com/epicenter/2011/05/netflix-traffic/
53. www.guardian.co.uk/film/2010/jul/31/dvd-sequels-lost-boys-3
54. Burg, *SAW VI* DVD commentary, 2010

CRITICAL RECEPTION

Critical acclaim for the SAW films is rare. *The New York Times* regarded the series as 'distasteful',[55] while the *LA Times* went as far as to say the films were 'vile filth'.[56] Perhaps it is worth remembering that such a vociferous response is possibly due to *SAW*'s very success; as the series has developed, it has increasingly become a mainstream concern, breaking out of the niche horror ghetto.

Although there are notable critics who support the horror genre – Kim Newman, Mark Kermode, Alan Jones – horror is usually dealt short shrift by critical institutions. Christopher Tookey of the *Daily Mail* implied that *Hostel* was the 'most violent pornography ever to have polluted mainstream cinema',[57] implying that the genre itself is somehow lesser than the rest of the cinematic canon, and that its more extreme texts bring the entire medium into disrepute. Certainly, reviews of horror films within the mainstream press would seem inclined to evaluate the film's morality, rather than any artistic or dramatic achievement. *The Sunday Times* review of *SAW 3D* wrings hands over the '18'-rated film's potentially adolescent audience – 'Your kids may be telling you they are going to see *Harry Potter*, in fact, they are getting off on buzzsaws'[58] – in an example of the lazy scaremongering that is typical of horror reception. The reviewer neglects to explain how, if 'our' kids were all 'getting off' on buzzsaws, the *Harry Potter* film (*The Deathly Hallows Pt. 1* [2010]) managed to out-gross *SAW 3D* to the tune of $766,329,827.

An interesting aspect of horror reception, however, is that the genre would seem to be critic proof. Horror audiences are mistrusting of, and even actively contradict, mainstream disparagement of their beloved genre. Despite initial maulings from mainstream reviewers, *SAW* and, indeed, *Hostel* went on to considerable success. A communication model called the 'two-step flow', postulated by sociologist Paul Lazarsfeld, suggests that ideas regarding the media 'flow' from opinion leaders to the wider population, are based on the trust placed in the ostensible media literacy and understanding of the opinion leader. However, this model (reviewer gives text poor review; film suffers accordingly) would seem to be inapplicable to horror fans. In an early review, one of America's most influential critics, Roger Ebert, soberly judged the original *SAW* 'an efficiently made thriller, cheerfully gruesome', but ultimately, 'not quite worth the ordeal it puts us through'. Tellingly, however, Ebert identifies that 'horror fans may forgive its contrivances',[59] propagating the disparaging received wisdom that horror fans are a breed apart within cinema audiences.

However, there is fan-specific media that is concerned with the consumption of horror. Even before the internet and its multitude of genre-specific forums, there was a thriving fanzine culture surrounding horror; *Cinema Sewer* was representative of this community, as was/is *Psychotronic*. Fans have created their own subculture, subverting conventional modes of acceptance and reception, fitting for such an abject, outsider genre. Perhaps the reviews that do matter to horror fans can be found on websites devoted to the genre. *Bloodydisgusting.com* is perhaps the 'biggest' and certainly most trusted of the horror sites. The site was very positive about *SAW*, one reviewer claming that *SAW* was 'a truly enticing film with one of the cleverest premises I've seen in a long time',[60] while another claimed that the distribution of *SAW* was 'by far Lionsgate's most brilliant decision in the company's entire history … *SAW* is the best horror film of 2004'. While this may read as typical fan hyperbole, it is important to remember that while the reviewers of *bloodydisgusting* are inclined to excitement, not all praise is given out so easily: fans can be the harshest critics of all. Their review of *SAW V* was not so positive, for example: '*SAW V* attempts to make the audience feel smart for sticking along for so long, only when it's all said and done you'll feel like a fool for sitting through this disappointment.'[61] The fan community that exists outside mainstream critical bodies provides an active, alternative forum for audiences to discuss texts, allowing horror to thrive within niche quarters.

FOOTNOTES

55. www.movies.nytimes.com/2004/10/29/movies/29saw.html
56. www.guardian.co.uk/film/2009/oct/15/saw-horror-movie-franchise
57. Tookey, *Daily Mail*, 24 March 2006
58. www.thesundaytimes.co.uk/sto/news/ireland/News/Comment/article433687.ece
59. www. rogerebert.suntimes.com/apps/pbcs.dll/article? AID=/20041028/ REVIEWS/40923005/1023
60. www.bloodydisgustingcom.saw
61. www.bloodydisgusting.com saw v

GAME OVER?

> I want people to be able to recognise a Wan–Whannell film. I want people to get to
> the point – like a Tim Burton movie or a John Woo movie – where they can just tell.
> Leigh Whannell[62]

While the box-office return for SAW V was a healthy $113,864,059, SAW VI managed just
$61,259,697. Compared to the money made by the first three, these diminishing returns
are not numbers in which Lionsgate can realistically have confidence. SAW 3D did spike
with $136,150,434; however, by this time, Lionsgate had all but given up on the franchise,
putting the narrative eggs of two intended forthcoming SAW films in the 3D basket
instead. It is tempting to argue that the new technology the film offered novelty for
audiences: a fitting last hurrah for the SAW franchise, but ultimately a one-off experience.
There is no evidence to suggest that the 3D format is an entirely bankable quantity yet
(reportedly, the returns for 2011's 3D releases of Pirates of the Caribbean 4 and Kung
Fu Panda 2 have disappointed the industry[63]), and that SAW's fallen star is incontestable.
There are the avenues of direct-to-video sequelisation open to the franchise, as is the
probable option of a reboot. However, at the time of writing, the above figures would
seem to make it 'game over' for the franchise. Indeed, SAW 3D was advertised as 'the
final SAW'. The idea of a conclusive sequel must always be taken with a pinch of salt,
though; Friday the 13th had it's 'final' chapter in 1984, and seven more sequels followed,
while the tagline for Nightmare on Elm Street's Part 6 announced that 'Freddy's Dead';
but we saw him again twice before the 2010 reboot. Like rock stars disingenuously
announcing a 'farewell tour', the terminal sequel is a last gamble, with its attention-
seeking USP that may just revive the fortunes of the ailing franchise. And, in fairness,
SAW 3D has doubled the performance of SAW VI's series low; but whether this is due to
a genuinely renewed audience interest or simply the fleeting novelty value of 3D (and
the proposed conclusion), is a matter for Lionsgate to decide.

Certainly, just as audiences grew weary of torture porn's antecedent, the Rape and
Revenge cycle, the subgenre that SAW spearheaded has dropped drastically out of
fashion. The Collector (2009) was a film marketed on its close links to SAW – writer-
directors Patrick Melton and Marcus Dunstan authored SAW sequels – and featured

similar abject concerns, with a family prisoner in a booby-trapped house. Unable to muster any sort of moral condemnation, *The Guardian* called it 'boring as hell',[64] and *The Hollywood Reporter* sighed, 'by this stage in the torture porn game, the prevailing sensation is a case of been there, impaled it'.[65] Gone are the days of outrage concerning torture porn. Instead, contemporary reception shrugs, 'We've seen it all before'. Perhaps the censorship of *A Serbian Film* (2010) (released with cuts) and *The Human Centipede 2* (2011) (eventually released with cuts after initially being refused a UK certificate) is symptomatic of the genre's redundancy: attention-seeking films that simply attempt to escalate their shock factor, while achieving very little else in terms of their impact. *A Serbian Film* is an interesting film in some ways, but its notorious 'newborn porn' scene is not controversial, just stupid and desperate.

What of the originators of the franchise, James Wan and Leigh Whannell? Despite the success and influence of their first film, they, somehow, do not benefit from the same brand-name recognition that their torture porn contemporaries Eli Roth, or even Rob Zombie, enjoy, despite their being film-makers whose achievements do not rival *SAW*'s in terms of box office impact. Is there a case to be made that the duo are nascent auteurs? We can certainly see similarities between *SAW* and their second feature, *Dead Silence* (released two years later, in 2006). Most analogous of these similarities is that *Dead Silence* features a murderous doll; but there is also a procedural aspect to the film (with Donnie Whalberg returning to repeat an Eric Matthews-style role), along with characteristic use of lighting and confined space. *Death Sentence*, Wan's 2007 updating of 1970s *Death Wish*-style (1974) revenge narratives, also has themes of retribution in common with *SAW*.

What is apparent is that, until 2011, the director and writer of the original *SAW*, although retaining an executive producer title on the sequels, have never quite achieved the commercial or critical success that they enjoyed with their initial collaboration. However, through Alliance Films and Stage 6 Films, early 2011 saw the pair release *Insidious*.

INSIDIOUS

In 1942, Val Lewton directed *Cat People*, the influential horror text that coined the genre

Insidious 2010

trope 'the bus'. 'The bus' is the term used to describe the sequence in a horror film that builds to and creates the sudden sounds or visuals within the film's diegesis that causes an involuntary reactive spasm, or 'jump', in the audience. During a typically atmospheric scene in *Cat People*, we follow the film's heroine as she walks down a shadowed street; the camera, lighting and score suggest that she is being followed… Suspenseful tension builds and builds, until, suddenly, it is interrupted by the 'jump' of a bus pulling abruptly and noisily into the scene. However trite or manipulative subsequent 'buses' have been (the head falling out of the sunken boat in *Jaws*, Carrie's hand reaching from the grave), the 'jump' response is evidence of our close physical relationship with horror: in response to artificial screen horrors, we goosebump, we scream, we jump. 2011's *Insidious* is James Wan's homage to 'the bus'; a supernatural horror that exploits every trick in the haunted house handbook, keeping its audience in the kind of carnival suspense one would enjoy upon a well-maintained ghost train.

> You can't escape the fact that things aren't worth what they were. Buildings previously worth millions are now not even worth the paper that the property developers selling them previously covered in outright lies.
> Stewart Lee[66]

At the Kapow Comic Convention in 2011, Whannell joked that he and Wan made films about 'what scares [them] the most… these days, it's bills' – a clear reference to a beleaguered economic climate, in which employment opportunities are diminishing, and, due to the stagnant housing market, our very homes have become a primary concern; difficult to uphold, impossible to sell. The plot of *Insidious* concerns a young family, who, on moving to a new home are terrorised by ghosts, following the mysterious coma of their little boy. While *SAW* was typical of post 9/11 horror, *Insidious* is firmly within the tradition of recession-era scares. Just as torture porn addressed (however obliquely) the anxieties concerning and iconography pertaining to the War on Terror, recession-era horror (*Sub-Prime Supernaturals? Economic Crisis Creepers?*) is rooted within the majority reaction to the financial crisis with its roots in the 2008 crash: confusion and growing dread. These texts foreground families, are set in their recognisably middle-class households, and concern forces beyond our mortal control and understanding that threaten to ruin these domestic set-ups (surely part of the auxiliary chill of *Paranormal Activity* for 2009 audiences was wondering how the haunting would affect the property's resale value?). In a sense, these films are an update of the haunted house trope, with a modern emphasis on technology: *Paranormal Activity 2* features extensive use of home CCTV footage, a security gesture that does precious little to protect the family from a force that proves to be as inevitable as it is terrible.

In 'recession horror' there is often the implication that the house, nominally a sanctuary, has become unreceptive, a problem in itself: you can't live in it, can't live without it. An attempt at escaping the toxic residence usually occurs within the logic of the narrative. *Insidious* features not just one, but two 'moves'; one before the narrative of the film, the other a response to the initial haunting. Consequently, the *mise-en-scène* features iconography of cardboard boxes and piles of 'stuff'; the detritus of domestic transit. There is never the sense that the habitat is settled. The film's resolutely old-school credits (a feature of *Insidious* that is abundantly evident is the creators' clear affection for horror tradition) is a monochrome sequence of fades featuring the original home's interiors; some blotted with hauntings (cloven footsteps across the wooden floor, a shadow in the kitchen), which serves to establish the 'haunted house' theme before we are even introduced to the characters. Scenes of domestic invasion constitute the scares: a burglar alarm soundtracks an unseen trespasser, a Dickensian boy interrupts a record player as the mother goes about domestic chores, and, in the film's climax, a pale hand shoots from a drawer, ghosts tumble from closets, the house shakes. Like *SAW, Insidious* depicts a hostile environment. However, unlike those of its forbearer, its interiors are not the lurid, neon-shaded chambers of old, but the ostensible safety of a typical family household.

Insidious shares creative talent with *Paranormal Activity*; Oren Peli, the latter's director, is *Insidious*' producer. This heritage is evident in the films' shared concerns of 'real-life' milieus and the supernatural activity within them. However, within the film's style and thematic relevance, the presence of Wan and Whannell is unmistakable. Although the post-*giallo* lighting codes are jettisoned (save for a throbbing red 'Further' in the film's finale), Wan's expressive use of space is still palpable; during the majestic sweep of a tracking shot as Renai's record is skipped, or creating the tight kitchen chaos of a pre-school morning. Whannell's script centres on a middle-class family in disarray: while Josh does not stray like Dr Gordon, there is the implication that he is distracted and vain (plucking a pesky grey hair, rubbing in eye cream before sleep); the film's emotional centre is a woman, Renai, played with wide-eyed horror by Rose Byrne. The second half of the film hinges on a twist that encourages repeat viewings, which has led to intriguing fan theories as to the nature of *who* exactly is doing the haunting in the film (similar to the obsessive *SAW* fan's hunt for clues and hints within the film and its sequels).

Within a month of its domestic release, *Insidious* had grossed $45 million: a handsome return for a low-budget horror. From a reported budget of $1.5 million, the film has gone on to gross $87 million globally. The film's distributor suggested that the film's success was due to the film being 'creepy and scary in a way that stays with you … It plays off of everyone's imagination'.[67] This is apparent. However, what is successful in terms of *Insidious* as a genre production is the *way* it is scary, the *exact* fears that it exploits *in order to* play off the imagination. The most entrepreneurial of genres, horror constantly evolves, adapting to the culture. The torture porn texts that explored the (tight, rancid) genre space that *SAW* opened up are now exhausted, 'old hat' horror cinema. It is the providence of commerce to exploit and repeat business models. However, perhaps this is not the policy of horror, which demands novelty in its subject matter, nourishing its subtexts upon new and fresh fears in the keen manner of a vampire feeding from virgin blood. In *SAW*, shackled, fearful victims gave a shivery frisson of contemporary relevance: now, the trope has suffered from blunting repetition.

For horror to work properly, it demands we take it seriously: however, an intense focus is difficult to maintain over seven films (not to mention a theme park ride …). Perhaps the reason horror is so ripe for parody (recall the *Scary Movie* franchise [2000-2006]), is that the films exclude any sense of self awareness, regarding themselves with total, grim earnestness: a limited position. Thus, in order to remain relevant, *Insidious* discards *SAW's* gothic-disco *mise-en-scène* and focuses on bodily suffering, returning to the most primal of horror tropes (the demon), and the aural tradition of the ghost story, repackaging the conventions for 2011's fraught financial landscape, where horror is all close to home. There is an appealing congruity with a film like *Insidious*, with its relatively miniscule budget, performing so well in such a parsimonious economy. James Wan even explicitly boasted of the film's budget in publicity - 'If you do it right', Wan said, 'a lot of the time you don't need a lot of money'.[68]

If the measure of an auteur is to create a recognisable style and thematic approach within consecutive cinema product, which is consistently applied to and developed across texts that are varied in terms of their plot and content, then *Insidious* would support Wan and Whannell's claim to the label. While it would seem that they have yet to make the transition to the brand-name status of some of their contemporaries, with their three films they have created a body of work that is in parts dazzling and intriguing, but whose Gothic charisma is always positioned to confront contemporary anxieties. Whannell's candid admission to making films about what scares Wan and himself is promising: there is no shortage of dark materials in our contemporary society, with its ruptured economy, and destabilising ongoing conflicts in the Middle East. Horror fans should hope that the two continue to be terrified, repositioning our own fears and anxieties through the dark filter of the screen, inspiring what will surely be a dark and dazzling legacy within contemporary horror cinema.

FOOTNOTES

62. www.guardian.co.uk/film/2011/apr/23/james-wan-leigh-whannell-insidious

63. www.nytimes.com/2011/05/30/business/media/30panda.html?_r=2&scp=1&sq=3-d%20 starts%20to%20fizzle%20and%20hollywood%20frets&st=cse

64. www.guardian.co.uk/film/2010/jun/24/the-collector-film-review

65. www.pastdeadline.com/hr/film-reviews/the-collector-film-review-1003999313.story

66. *Stewart Lee's Comedy Vehicle*, 2009

67. www.boxofficemojo.com/movies/?id=insidious.htm

68. www.walletpop.com/2011/03/29/saw-director-james-wan-spills-gory-details-about-cost-cutting/

BIBLIOGRAPHY

Alcock, N. "Boo-hoo I'm Trapped" is the New "Boo-hoo I'm a Vampire". Alcock,
    www.theincrediblesuit.blogspot.com/2010/09/boo-hoo-im-trapped-is-new-boo-hoo-im.html

Anon. 'Film fans faint at *SAW III* show.' www.news.bbc.co.uk/2/hi/6101704.stm

Anon. *SAW* DVD. www.bbfc.co.uk/BVF201470/

Barnes, B. and Ciephly, M. '3-D Starts to Fizzle, and Hollywood Frets', *The New York Times*.
    www.nytimes.com/2011/05/30/business/media/30panda.html?_r=2&scp=1&sq=3-d%20
    starts%20to%20fizzle%20and%20hollywood%20frets&st=cse

Biskind, P. *Easy Riders, Raging Bulls*, London: Bloomsbury, 1998.

Bradshaw, P. The Collector review, *The Guardian*. www.guardian.co.uk/film/2010/jun/24/the-collector-
    film-review

Cashmore, P. 'Will this new movie kill off torture porn for good?', *The Guardian*. www.guardian.co.uk/
    film/2010/aug/28/torture-porn-frightfest-quiz

Clover, Carol. *Men Women and Chainsaws: Gender in the Modern Horror Film*, New York: Princeton
    University Press, 1993.

Dicker, R. 'SAW director James Wan Spills Gorty Details about Cost-Cutting', *Daily Finance*. www.
    walletpop.com/2011/03/29/saw-director-james-wan-spills-gory-details-about-cost-cutting/

Ebert, R. *SAW* review. rogerebert.suntimes.com/apps/pbcs.dll/article?AID=/20041028/
    REVIEWS/40923005/1023

Edelstein, D. 'Now Playing at Your Local Multiplex: Torture Porn', *New York Magazine*. www.nymag.
    com/movies/features/15622/

Freud, S. 'The Uncanny' The Standard Edition of Complete Psychological Works of Sigmund Freud,
    Vol XVII 1919.

Gilbert, A. 'Elwes Sues Saw', *Joblo.com*. www.joblo.com/horror-movies/news/elwes-sues-saw

Gilmore, G. Quoted in: www.lionsgatepublicity.com/epk/saw5/docs/pro_notes.doc

Godfrey, A. 'American Pie 7 Donnie Darko 2', *The Guardian*. www.guardian.co.uk/film/2010/jul/31/
    dvd-sequels-lost-boys-3

Graham, J. 'SAW: brutality is only skin deep', *The Guardian*. www.guardian.co.uk/film/2009/oct/15/
    saw-horror-movie-franchise

Guiness Book of World Records, Guiness World Books, USA: 2010

Hari, J. 'I Saw *SAW III* – and Survived.' http://johannhari.com/2006/page/4/

Holden, S. SAW review, *The New York Times*. reviewwww.movies.nytimes.com/2004/10/29/movies/29saw.html

Ide, W. www.entertainment.timesonline.co.uk/tol/arts_and.../film/article6964114.ece

Jones, A. *The Rough Guide to Horror Movies*, London: Penguin, 2005, p36

Kerekes, D. and Slater, D. *See No Evil Banned Films and Video Controversy*, Manchester: Head Press.

Kermode, M. 'I was a Teenage Horror Fan: or, How I Learnt to Stop Worrying and Love Linda Blair', in Barker, M. and Petley, J. *Ill Effects: The Media/Violence Debate*. London: Routledge, 1997.

King, S. *Danse Macabre*, London: Futura, 1981.

McClintock, P. 'Lionsgate: The Hidden Enigma', *Variety*. www.variety.com/article/VR1117942674?refcatid=13&printerfriendly=true

Newman, K. *The BFI Companion to Horror*, London: BFI, 1996.

Osmond, A. *SAW* review in *Sight and Sound Volume 14 Issue 12*, London: BFI, December 2004

Paglia, C. *Sexual Persona*, London: Penguin, 1992.

Poe, E. A. *Great Short Works of Poe* ed. Thompson, G.R. New York.

Poe, E. A. *Spirits of the Dead: Tales and Poems*, London: Penguin, 1997.

Queenan, J. 'Joe Queenan's guide to horror film clichés', *The Guardian*. www.guardian.co.uk/film/2010/oct/22/queenan-horror-cliches-ring

Rechtshaffen, M. The Collector review, *The Hollywood Reporter*. www.pastdeadline.com/hr/film-reviews/the-collector-film-review-1003999313.story

Rose, J. *Beyond Hammer: British Horror Cinema Since 1970*, Leighton Buzzard: Auteur Publishing, 2009.

Singel, R. 'Netflix Beats BitTorrent's Bandwidth', *Wired*. www.wired.com/epicenter/2011/05/netflix-traffic/

Tookey, Christopher, *Hostel* review in *Daily Mail*, 24th March 2006.

Tudor, A. *Monsters and Mad Scientists*, Oxford: Blackwell, 1989.

Wan, J. and Whannell, L. *SAW* screenplay. www.imsdb.com/Movie%20Scripts/Saw%20Script.html

Welsh, L. *The Cutting Room*, Edinburgh: Canongate, 2002.

Williams, L. 'When the Woman Look's, from Doane, M. A., Mellancamp, P. and Williams, L. eds, *Re-Vision: Essays in Feminist Film Criticism* Los Angeles, American Film Institute.

Wise, D. 'Are *SAW* creators James Wan and Leigh Whannell returning to their low-budget roots with Insidious?' *The Guardian*. www.guardian.co.uk/film/2011/apr/23/james-wan-leigh-whannell-insidious

Wood, R. 'The American Nightmare: Horror in the 70s', in Jancovich, Mark *Horror: The Film Reader* London: Routledge 2002.

Zuckerman, M. 'What is Sensory Deprivation?', *Big Think*. www.bigthink.com/ideas/17531

"Anne Billson offers an accessible, lively but thoughtful take on the '80s-set Swedish vampire belter... a fun, stimulating exploration of a modern masterpiece. ****"

Empire

"[Anne Billson's] tight-packed monograph ... is fang-sharp and sensitive... ****"

Total Film

Also in this series

DEVIL'S ADVOCATES

WITCHFINDER GENERAL

IAN COOPER

Beyond Hammer

British Horror Cinema Since 1970

James Rose